# EARN A BLACKBELT IN...

## AN AVERAGE GUY'S GUIDE TO LIFE

## ROBERT NICHOLS

Elite
PUBLICATIONS

All attempts have been made to ensure the accuracy of the information presented in this book, but this is not a guarantee.

Earn a Blackbelt In...An Average Guy's Guide to Life
All Rights Reserved
Copyright © 2022 by Robert Nichols
First Printing: April 2022

This book may not be reproduced, transmitted, or stored in whole or in part by any means, including graphic, electronic, or mechanical without the express written consent of the publisher except in the case of brief quotations embodied in critical articles and reviews.

If you would like to do any of the above, please seek permission by Elite Publications at +1 919-618-8075 or via email to info@elitepublications.org

Publisher: Elite Publications
Language: English
Library of Congress Control Number: 2022907596
Paperback ISBN: 978-1-958037-03-4
eBook ISBN: 978-1-958037-04-1
Kindle Version Available
Imprint: Independently published
Book Cover and Interior design by: Tiger Shark, Inc.

PRINTED IN THE UNITED STATES OF AMERICA

*Dedicated to*

To my Wife: for helping me believe in myself.

To my Mother: for teaching me hard work.

To my Father: for teaching me perseverance.

To the OG's for helping me build the beginning.

To the Wolfpack for helping me build the future.

To my daughter for being my WHY.

# TABLE OF CONTENTS

# FOREWORD

So...you've picked my book.

Thanks. I mean that. You might have picked it up because you know me in some manner and know that I'm the type of person who always has something to say. Maybe you picked it up because you know me professionally and again, you know I've got a lot to say. Or maybe you just happened to come across it and it piqued your interest.

Let's get a couple things straight, whatever the reason.

First and foremost, I am not an expert on any of the topics discussed in this book. Hell, this is my 1st book so I don't know if I'm much of a writer either. I'm an average everyday person like most. And by that, I mean I've got a full-time job and stress about paying bills sometimes. I do my best to just keep everyone at home happy and enjoy a beer with friends. I've got a teenage daughter that I can barely keep up with half the things she's talking about. My wife and I like to go out to dinner and watch bad reality tv. I'm not saying I'm not a happy person with my life. I very much am, but as I said, I think I'm a pretty average guy.

Who knows, maybe after this book some might consider me an expert, but I certainly don't. I am a guy that's done well in life. I say that being only 43 at the time of writing this, but still. I've gotten to do some pretty cool things and travel and have some cool experiences.

And I will completely admit, I've made a lot of mistakes and screwed up a lot of things. But I think one thing that I've been fortunate with is that I'm pretty good about learning from those mistakes. So, I guess that's kind of the point of this book. Here are some mistakes I've made in certain areas and what I've learned from them. An average guy.

Second, this isn't a book about martial arts. Sorry if it comes as a surprise given the title, and a surprise because, yes, that is what I do for a living. I am a martial arts instructor. I've been training for more than 30 years and running a school for more than 20. I have black belts, accolades, hall of fame inductions, trophies, and all of that. But, to be honest, so do a lot of instructors.

A good instructor, in my opinion, must be willing to admit that they don't know everything and that there is still a lot to learn. I'm not necessarily referring to punching and kicking. I'm referring to your efforts to better yourself as a person. Learning about how to educate, lead, read people, and motivate others.

This isn't "How to" Earn a Black Belt in…

You should think of it more as "Why you should" Earn a Black Belt in…

Also, here's a spoiler. The next word will not be karate, taekwondo, jujitsu, or any other martial art.

Please don't misunderstand me. Martial arts is something I suggest to almost everyone. It's a fantastic tool for personal growth and development. Martial arts has aided in the development of my life. And while I will mention martial arts and discuss them in this book, it is not about them.

Finally, you should read this book as though we were sitting in a room having a conversation. Not me telling you how to live your life as you read these pages. Please don't listen to me. Listen to yourself.

When two people converse, they can give each other advice. You can be motivated in a variety of ways. As you hear about someone else's life, you can be reflective and have ideas about your own. Some people may claim they aren't readers, so think of this as a conversation between two people rather than a book.

So, if I make a point that resonates with you, stop and ask yourself why. If you completely disagree, do the same thing. Why do you disagree? If I ask a question, it's because I'm interested in hearing the answer, so you should stop and formulate one in your head.

I've read a lot of motivational and self-help books. I've read some really great ones that I've gotten a lot out of, and I've read some that I got maybe one thing out of 400 pages. Some of those books (but by no means all) are hard to read because they read like directions. But we aren't building furniture here. Everyone's path is different. So, if we can have a conversation and provoke thoughts, I think we can all get something more out of this.

Again, thanks for picking up my book. This is a new experience for me. I've spent years teaching martial arts, and that comes with the responsibility of motivating others. Telling stories that inspire others to strive harder and achieve more. With that also comes me having to reflect and grow just as much as I ask others to. I hope you get as much out of this book as I did in writing it.

# INTRODUCTION

There are a few things that come to mind when I think of a book's introduction. First and foremost, it establishes what the book will be about and gives you a sense of what you will find inside.

The knowledge and opinions of a black belt going through life. That's absolutely part of it. However, it's also the opinion of a regular person. At least that's how I think of myself. I'm just trying to live my life on this rock like everyone else. Have a good time, take care of my loved ones, pay my bills. It's the black belt side of me that has developed the ability to make an impact on others.

So, as we look at this journey, this is a book that will include some personal stories that relate to the lessons in the chapters. So, I feel like I should give you a little background on me.

I was born in High Bridge, New Jersey. A small town in west Jersey. Although anyone from Jersey knows we only recognize north and south. So, let's say north. I was born in 78' so I grew up in the 80's and 90's. Come on now, the best time. The music, movies, tv shows. The nostalgia of the era hits hard. No internet, no cell phones, just staying out until the street lights came on, or in the teen years, just didn't come home at all.

I understand that everyone grows up differently. Everyone has a story to tell, and many people have had it worse than me. But my experiences are what have made me who I am. My parents divorced before I can even remember. We grew up relatively poor. I say relatively as in yes, I had a roof over my head, but my mom used to like to say if we had bread and the neighbor had peanut butter then we ate pretty well. My Mother was a workhorse who gave it her all. I knew we were poor but I never went hungry. I never wanted for anything. She was probably the number one person who taught me in life the value of hard work. Though admittedly, I did not pick up on those lessons until much later in life.

A Little background on my parents. Mom was a Marine. I don't mean like, yea she served, I mean she served in the 1st female battalion ever to train on Parris Island. She served from 72' to 78'. And if you remember correctly, I was born in 78'. See what happened there. She raised me on her own. Sometime around 91' she suffered 4 brain aneurysms. Seeing or talking to her today you would never know she went through something that should have killed her. She's just that tough. But until the aneurysms she raised me on the tips of a waitress in a truck stop. I don't think I ever heard her complain. She just did what needed done.

My father was a cop, and sometime in 77', he pulled over to help Mom with a flat tire. That's how they met. In 2021 after not really speaking for 35 years Mom told Dad she purposefully let the air out of her tire so he would stop and help her. Yes, I said after not speaking for some years. Finding that out after all those years he was madder that he got his uniform dirty then that she tricked him.  The long and short is Mom left the core, I was born, and they divorced soon after.

After my Father was a cop for many years, he was then a long haul trucker.  And he has always been a biker. I mean old school, Harley chopper riding, MC club belonging biker. He's such a legend in that world that I think he's been riding longer than he could even walk. For all the reasons that life goes the way it does, I can say I didn't see him a lot growing up. We did not have much of a relationship. However, in the last few years, he and I have grown incredibly close and I've learned a great number of lessons from him as well. More on that in future chapters.

I was also a tiny kid with no direction, no confidence, and no drive. I was bullied in school like most small, awkward kids in the 80's. Not much really changed by high school other than I got more depressed and angrier. I was the punk rocker that didn't care much for school. We didn't have emo kids back then, but you get the idea. Fighting wasn't uncommon but I was mostly able to stay out of trouble. Somehow, I passed all my classes and even graduated on time. I did have some moments of success. I was good at art. I was on the fencing team. My senior year, I was even captain, which gave me my first experience of leadership. But, like many others, I found high school to be a lonely and miserable time. In the early 90's teen boys weren't exactly known for dealing with their feelings well. Especially ones that had a lack of confidence, depression, and no people skills. I was also an angry kid. Man did I have anger. In the 80's and 90's getting into a scrap wasn't a big deal. If you were picked on in school you were expected to just stand up for yourself. And I had a lot of anger to put into that.

College wasn't very noteworthy. I had a full-time job working at a supermarket and it took me 5 years to get my 2-year degree. Those years were the normal college stuff. Parties and wasting a lot of time and money.

I always say college was the 5 years I needed to grow up. Unbelievable that I went to community college at all. I owed that motivation to one of my fencing coaches. A man that saw things in me that I didn't. That literally took me out of class one day and drove me to college to enroll.

However, with college I racked up some debt. At that age money honestly didn't really have much meaning. I worked and spent. College was put on credit cards and forgotten about. I was clearly on my way to a less than great existence without a care in the world. Not a direction either. I had little sense of focus or a future.

So where did the martial arts come in? I started training at 12. It was very sporadic and off and on until I was about 20. Being on the fencing team and the support I got from coaches helped. It probably kept me from quitting everything. I didn't take my martial arts training seriously until I was older. I wish I had taken it more seriously during those teenage years. Between martial arts and fencing I would have been much more focused. Eventually I moved on from fencing and once I could afford martial arts classes myself, I really started training hard. Started gaining a little focus. Spending more time around positive people. The community that comes with belonging to a martial arts school started to change things for me. I fell in love with the way classes and training made me feel. I became a sponge for information in class. Soaking up any new move or technique I could learn.

Martial arts really made me the person I am today. I don't think every person that studies has this experience. For most it's a hobby. But for me it became a calling. I don't think of myself as an amazing martial artist. I really don't. I think I'm pretty good. Very solid since it's my profession. But I'm no Bruce Lee or pro UFC fighter. What I am is a great teacher. I'm a motivator. I'm good with people. I'm very fortunate to have developed these skills.

So now you've got a little background on me. Like I said earlier, this should be a bit of a conversation, so before we get into anything else let's do two things.

Take a minute to think about what your background is. If we are going to start getting motivated and work on ourselves then we have to know where we've been. Where you came from. What baggage you're still carrying. Where you want to go. What you know in your heart you are good at, and even where you fall short. To do this you've gotta be honest.

Real honest.

Be honest with yourself about where you've been and where you are. What brought you to this point? What's good about it and what's bad. Did you learn from the screw ups and the negatives? If you didn't, could you now? It's never too late to learn a lesson. Don't be afraid to be vulnerable. That's the only way you are going to work toward being the person you want to be. It's hard to be honest with yourself sometimes. Especially if you aren't going to like the truth. But if you want to grow, you've got to do it.

The thing about growth is this: It's never going to stop. It can be a little or a lot. Good or bad. It can go in directions you didn't expect and even ones you didn't want. One day you can wake up and wonder how you get to this point. In a bad place or a good place. But as long as you are willing to do it, to put in the work, you can grow and evolve. In the best way possible. You are in control of it.

If your goal is to cut the grass, what do you do? You prep. You check the weather, pick up debris in the yard, make sure you got gas for the mower. Then you fire that sucker up and get to work. A few hours later. Mission accomplished. Good job. Grab a beer, you've earned it.

But the problem is, the grass starts growing again right away. The goal needs to be reset or adjusted. This is where the process of growth takes place. In the successes, setbacks, and adjustments.

Now, let's define "black belt." One of my instructors used to say a black belt is the "master of basic techniques." But just like that grass you cut, there's still going to be room to grow. I think a common misconception that people have is that you work to earn a black belt and then that's it. There's nothing else. You're now a black belt. And unfortunately, many people think that's it. It's over.

I don't think that could be further from the truth. I've always thought that you can't even really call yourself a black belt until you've actually had a black belt rank longer than you had your colored belt rank. And of course, put in the effort. To me earning a black belt really just means you've gotten the basics down so you can really start to fine-tune them and learn. Because once you're a black belt the point is to apply the lessons you learned along the way to other areas of your life. The focus, discipline, drive. You aren't going to put in the effort to get your driver's license and then never drive, are you? Or learn the alphabet but never learn to put together words, sentences, paragraphs, stories. You get the basics down then you apply the lessons. Hopefully to a mastery level.

So, if we define the black belt as a certain level of mastery of a skill, then you could even argue or say that a doctor is basically a black belt of medicine. Just like a person who's been a carpenter for 25 years is definitely a master of their craft. A black belt in their field. They have gotten down the lessons and then spent the time applying them. Mastering them. Yes, some are better than others, but the tools and the mindset are there.

Just like a black belt in martial arts, these people don't stop learning. New technologies are developed, changes in their fields that they have to learn about. Even as they continue to grow older and gain experience, they have to make adjustments as well. So, to me, this is what it means to be a black belt. Continuing to make those changes, continuing to grow, and continuing to evolve on those paths.

I often tell my students that you are only as good as your last class. You can be a black belt and come in the class and not work like one. You can also be a white belt and show up and work with the attitude of a black belt. I think this is a big part of this book, you're going to have good days and bad days, you're going to have setbacks, you're going to have areas that you wish you could've done better in, and you're going to have areas you feel super solid in. To earn a black belt and work toward mastering different areas of your life, you have to keep pushing forward and learning from your experiences. Even if you've already got a good handle on some of these areas. The grass still needs tending. Apply the things that you've learned and just keep trying to be better. Take the areas you want to improve in and do the work.

So, we've got a starting point. Ask questions as you read this. Question what my opinions are, form your own. Get ready to break a sweat, because it's time to go through these ranks and work on earning our black belts.

# CHAPTER ONE
# WHITE BELT

So white belt is the beginning. I'm not going to talk about my childhood anymore. Or even my early training. But the event that started me on my path. The big moment that was the start of the change for me was a painful one.

I was 22 years old, still working a supermarket job and still aimless as I was getting ready to wrap up college. I was pretty sure at that point I was going to go into law enforcement. I had some connections with some friends in a local police department and was in the process of applying for the police academy. A solid career path for anyone; and with martial arts training it seemed like a good choice. I was still training and taking class 3 to 4 times a week while spending time with friends and avoiding any real responsibility. Having an opportunity in law enforcement was a major opportunity for me. Although I didn't feel very passionate at the idea, I wasn't dumb enough to not take advantage of the opportunity.

Like many martial arts schools, we were a small community. Often you will find a group of unlikely friends ranging in age and backgrounds. Lots of different types of people are drawn to martial arts schools. Among my group of friends at the school was a man named Alan. Alan was the brother of one of the local cops, who also happened to be an old friend of our families. I knew his brother pretty well, so by extension, Alan and I became fast friends.

One afternoon Alan had invited me to go running and then get in some training. The only thing he loved more than martial arts was running. Alan and I had trained together for 2 years and at this point, extra training with the group was common. A chance to break a sweat and hang with friends.

Alan had been a police officer for several years until changing careers to be a firefighter. As a fireman he actually broke his back saving someone from a burning building. After healing he worked with mentally and physically handicapped children at a specialized hospital. He was kind, level headed, and respected for his wisdom. He was an overall great guy.

So, after a solid afternoon of working out and sparring in Alan's backyard, we were taking a break and enjoying a beer together.

At one point he said to me, "So I hear you're planning on going into the police Academy. "

"Yeah, planning on it. I think it's just the easiest thing for me to do right now. I don't know what else I would do honestly. "

Alan replied, "Don't do that. You're not a cop. I know you and it's not for you. "

A little surprised I looked at him, "Oh yeah? Well then what am I? "

"You're a martial arts teacher, "he replied. "I know you would be really good at this. You've got to trust me on this one. "

That was kind of the end of it. At the time being a martial arts instructor was nowhere in my mind for my future. After a bad experience coaching fencing, I honestly didn't want to teach anything. I went about my day and went home and didn't really think much of the conversation. I appreciated his advice but being a thickheaded 22-year-old, I don't think it really stuck with me at the time.

The next day was like any other, I went to work and afterwards ended up going out with friends. At about 1130pm I got a call from my mother telling me to come home. A mutual friend of mine and Alan's who also happened to be a police officer was waiting for me. He had something he needed to talk to me about. I honestly figured that he had gotten word of some stupid thing I had done and was going to chew me out for it but was being cool and didn't tell my mother. So, I didn't think much of it.

When I arrived home, he was leaning against his squad car. His eyes were already wrapped in tears. "I don't know how else to tell you. Alan is dead. He died of a heart attack this afternoon. "

It was a complete and utter shock. He was 41 years old and in the best shape of anybody I knew. I had seen him the day before. We trained. We talked. This was unreal. I think he was the first person I knew that died that I was close to. On an unusually warm November day he was out for a jog and had a heart attack.

Early the next morning we went over to Alan's brother's house to see him and pay our respects. I clearly remember walking in the front door and laying there on the couch was Alan's martial arts uniform. His brother intended to have him laid to rest in his uniform. He was given his black belt post mortem.

I spoke at his funeral. So did several other members of our school and the head instructor. Hundreds of people came to his funeral. I heard there was a multiple hour wait to pay your respects at his casket. That's what a good man he was. He didn't make an impression on other people; he made an impact.

The day after the funeral I removed my application from the police department and knew what I was going to do with my life. I went to my instructor and asked for a job. It was time to make a change, I had a direction and nothing was going to stop me from going in it.

It took something shocking to make me get my life on track and get focused. It took the loss of my friend to decide it was time to grow up and make something of myself.

Thank you, Alan.

# CHAPTER TWO

# EARN A BLACK BELT IN PERSONAL GROWTH

Isn't this why we read books like this? Because we want to grow, we want to evolve. We are looking for something different, or we are looking to change something about ourselves. We go through different stages in our lives and we have to adjust and grow in each of them.

When you're on an airplane and you're listening to those safety announcements come on in the beginning of the flight, what did they tell you? Be sure to put your own oxygen mask on before helping someone else.

You can't help other people to grow, you can't provide for other people, you can't be counted on by other people, until you make sure to have your stuff together too. Yes, there are plenty of people that help others and secretly their lives are falling apart. My mindset is we need to be genuine. For ourselves and others. Because once you've really got yourself sorted, you're going to be able to help others even more.

# BE WILLING TO CHANGE

So, to earn a black belt in personal growth we have to first be willing to make changes. I can't really tell you how big or small these changes are going to need to be. That's really got to be up to you and your situation. But you've got to be OK with change. For example, if you want to get in shape, you have to be willing to make changes to your diet and changes to your routine so you're getting more exercise. If you're not willing to make those changes, you're never going to get into the shape you want.

Yes, change can be scary. Yes, change can be hard. Making change and sticking with it is even harder. I've said on the workout floor before, "Everybody wants to be a black belt until it's time to train like one." Well, everybody wants to be in shape, and be happy, and make more money, and have positive relationships, and all these different things until they realize they're going to have to make changes and then stick with them. But massive action and taking risks is a requirement if we want to grow. Change won't happen without taking a few risks, emotionally and depending on the situation, physically as well. Courage is created through these actions. It builds momentum.

This ends up being an overwhelming idea because most people think that change has to be all or nothing. That it should be 100% changed right away. That's the problem, if you set yourself up with an overwhelming task, how are you ever going to achieve it? You don't stand at the bottom of Mt Everest and say, "ok, I'm going to the top." You make a plan to deal with all the little things that you will need to do and prepare to get there. You break down the endgame with smaller, more manageable parts.

You've got to think about making small amounts of change over a period of time. If you know you're not good at communication, you aren't just magically going to go out and start having in-depth conversations with people. Instead, you start by setting smaller goals. Start by saying "hello". Or just asking someone how their day is. When they open up to you, you've got to open up to them. You don't have to go crazy, but you're sharing a little bit and that's going to start to build your confidence. Then you build from there. No, that's not going to happen instantaneously or even be easy. If you want to change a behavior or build a skill it takes time and effort.

Any goal you want to achieve, anything you want to improve, any changes you want to make, have to be broken down into actionable steps. Whether that growth has to be done one percent at a time or 10% at the time. As long as there is progress, then you're on your way.

## HONEST SELF EVALUATION

Now, if you're willing to change, you also have to figure out what it is that you want to change. Or just improve on. You need to be clear on what you are looking to improve or change in order for growth to happen. I can't tell you what you need to change. That's where you have to be really honest with yourself. Take some time and have some serious introspection on the person you want to be or what areas of your life you are looking to improve on.

So, this requires some thought. Not just a quick, "Oh I need to have a better relationship with my partner".

Ok, so why do you? What are you doing that makes you feel that way? What can you do to make it better? How do they feel about this? What are you willing to compromise and what aren't you?

We can be really good at making excuses and lying to ourselves. Shifting the blame onto someone else or some external factor of why things are a certain way.

"I don't have time to work out."

"Oh, she's just being a jerk."

"My boss just likes that person better."

It's easier to have a reason why we can't do something then be honest about what we really need to do to get there. It's easier to just stay in our old patterns of behavior, to stay in our comfort zone, then to make real change.

Ok, fine. Maybe your boss doesn't like you. Maybe your partner was in a bad mood. Does doing a little soul searching really hurt? If we work on improving and growing in the areas we can control, we can influence some of those things we can't control.

The hard thing that comes with a solid self-evaluation is also looking at the things that we may not like about ourselves. Come on, no one is perfect. So, when we are doing these deep dives, we need to be honest about the areas we fall short. No matter how much we may not like the results. If we can't stand something about ourselves, how can we expect others to?

## CLEAN DEFINITIONS

Just like change needs to happen a little bit at a time over a long period, it also needs to be clearly defined so you know what directions you need to go. These can be redefined down the road, but if you don't know exactly what it is that you want to work on then you won't have a direction. And yes, when you do really sit and look at yourself you might find there are several areas you want to improve in. That's fine. You can prioritize if need be or really look at it and see if by improving one area you also improve another. For example, if you want to work on improving the relationships in your life and having more quality friendships you may realize that as you work on these areas it also improves your work life because you're a happier person and you learn how to interact with other people better. Or if you decide you're a very disorganized person and need to put some systems in place to be more efficient, that can easily affect your job, your time for hobbies, and your overall stress levels. Once you get organized in one area of your life, it's easier to get organized in every area of life.

You can't just say you want to change something about yourself and then magically it's going to happen. Making that decision to change might be the very first step, but there's got to be a lot more after that. By creating actionable steps, little things to be mindful about, what to do on a daily or weekly basis, you move forward in that goal of self-growth. Once you're motivated to start change and you get into the habit of taking whatever steps you've decided upon, discipline is what keeps you going. There doesn't even need to be an end goal. Self-growth isn't always something that has a tangible ending. Sure, it can, if it's moving careers or mending a broken relationship. But at the same time, it will then later be a goal that needs either readjusted or at least continually cultivated to keep whatever positive progress you made to keep going. Whatever it is though, define it, redefine it, and pivot when need be.

Setting goals may seem silly to some people but it gives you something to work toward. And the more clearly you define the goal the easier it is to see it, to visualize it. That's going to make it seem more real and make it more likely you are actually going to put in the work.

## CREATE A PLAN

You've gotta have a plan. We aren't talking about just deciding to go to the store and pick up a pizza. We are talking about making changes to parts of our behavior, or achieving something, improving something that we have put some serious time and thought into. So, a plan is a must. You can't just decide you want to do something. We have to act. If we are going to act, making a plan on what to do makes the most sense.

Make a list. What are you trying to accomplish? Let's say we are trying to improve our relationship with our spouse. What are your expectations? What things do you see that will support your outcome? Work backwards. When do things often go wrong? Or when do you not feel as close as you would like? Once you recognize the moments and opportunities, create actions to take at those times.

Gather your resources. Educate yourself while you're making your plan. Search online on the subject. Set up reminders. Discuss your plans with a friend and get their feedback. Point being make an intelligent plan of attack. Set yourself up for success.

Creating a plan isn't easy. No matter how much you plan, things can pop up to throw you off. Once you have your plan as set up as you can, implementing it can be even harder. However, it's better to have a plan then to just wing it. If you want to make change and go in without a plan it's going to fall apart fast. So, the more clearly defined your plans are, the more likely you can stick to it.

## CUT YOURSELF SOME SLACK SOMETIMES

You've made the decision that there is something you want to work on. You've been introspective and honest with yourself. You've got a game plan about how to proceed. You're going to be excited because you're gonna feel like you're making progress. So, what happens when there's a setback? I mean, we can't be expected to be perfect every single day of our lives.

We are humans, we all screw up. Sometimes it's small, sometimes it's large. But it happens. It might even be something that's completely out of our control. I am the first to admit I mess stuff up all the time. Monthly, weekly, daily. Some of the things that I work on growing and improving on don't happen every day. The day gets away from me and that goal falls short.

But you have to be OK with that. Just like accepting change, you have to accept that you're going to screw up and there are going to be setbacks. It shouldn't be that big of a deal. That's part of adjusting and reevaluating the game plan and moving forward. It's ok to have an off day. We all do. It's different though if that day turns into a week. Then something's really wrong.

I've got a list of 25 things on my daily personal to-do list. I don't remember the last time I got all 25 of them done in a day. But if I end up pulling off 20 or more, I feel pretty damn positive about my day. Whatever ones I did not do that day I try to make an effort to pick up on the next day. There is an ebb and flow to these things. Some days you're going to do great on a handful of your tasks and one or two might fall short of the mark. But then the next day you do great on those but something else slips.

Come on, life is spinning plates. You're trying to pay attention in one area and maybe another area falls a little short so you run over to pay attention to that and then you have to run back to another one then you realize, "oh man I completely forgot to deal with this thing over here" and run back. Yes, by making efforts to stick to your game plan you're gonna deal with all that a lot better. But the point is you've got to be OK with making these adjustments and going back-and-forth and improving in different areas at different rates of growth.

I'm sure most of us have heard the saying, "progress, not perfection."

I will give you another one. When I was a kid growing up in High Bridge there was a local barber shop where I got my haircut. Carl and Company Haircutters. Feels like the place has been there since the dawn of time. From my childhood I very clearly remember, Carl had a little piece of paper tucked into the top left corner of his mirror. And it said, "perfection is unattainable but, in its pursuit, we may achieve excellence." That quote has stuck with me for years. Perfection is just not realistic. But the pursuit of it gives us greatness.

A friend of mine gave me some solid advice. "Not everything is Black and White. If you want to succeed, you've got to learn to manage the gray."

Yes!

Manage the gray areas. If things are great, they are great. When things are bad, they are bad. But that's not life. Life is mostly in between. If you can learn to manage the in between times, working to keep things good, working to keep things from becoming bad, you are growing. When you fall to extremes, good or bad, you often set yourself up for a crash. If you work on managing the gray areas you are setting yourself more realistically.

The point is that whatever areas you are trying to grow and change in, cut yourself some slack. It's OK to screw up every now and then. Then you reevaluate, readjust, and move forward. That's what a black belt does.

## LIVE OUT LOUD

Don't feel like you need to keep these goals to yourself either. There's something to be said about sharing our goals and aspirations, or the things we want to be working on about ourselves, with other people. Yes of course, if it's a little too personal you don't have to go on Instagram and message out all your followers right away. If you've got a circle of friends in your life or even one person that you're OK talking to about why not share that goal or what you're working on. There's something to be said about just even saying it and putting it out there into the world. Also, you've got the tried-and-true idea of writing your goals down and putting them somewhere where you can see them.

When I'm working on something or going for something big, I always have a couple of people that I'm honest with and I talk to them about it. Because if I feel like I'm putting it out there and telling someone else about it, it becomes more real in my life. It also holds me accountable.

Who knows, those people that you share with, you may be surprised to learn they are working on things of their own. You may even inspire them to want to choose to grow in some area. If your chosen friend is working on their own growth then now you've got a friend on the path. It's comforting to know you aren't the only one trying to grow and improve.

For a while I was doing motivational videos and putting them on my Instagram story. I enjoy doing it but I'll totally admit that I kind of gassed out and stopped doing them. Then at random I would start to get messages from people I know telling me how much they really enjoy those videos and how I got them motivated every week when I put them out. So yes, I had to take a little bit of a deep breath. Reevaluate what I was doing and create a game plan so that I would get back into the habit of making those videos. The videos weren't just about me. When I learned they were inspiring others I felt a sense of responsibility to keep them consistent. I will completely admit that I struggle with getting them out sometimes, but knowing that there are now other people that enjoy them and look forward to them holds me a bit accountable to doing it.

Before you know it, you might end up having a small circle of people that are looking to do the same type of growth that you are. I've read examples and analogies in tons of books that all basically say if you hang out with four losers you're going to be the fifth. But if you hang out with four motivated and successful people, guess what you're going to end up being?

## CONSISTENCY

So now you've been doing all this stuff to work on improving yourself. You've been open to making a change; you've been really honest about yourself about what you want to work on. You've sat down and defined the goals and put them in actionable steps. You've been lenient with yourself when you make mistakes. You've tried to get some other people involved or at least put it out there in the world so you can move forward on it. Well, right there, to me that's personal growth. You're already doing it. I guess it's one of those things where sometimes the journey can be the destination.

You are going to hear a lot about consistency in this book. Get used to it. Consistency is going to be one of the keys to helping us in everything we are talking about and working on. All growth requires consistency. You can't develop new habits or break old ones without getting consistent at it. So set yourself up for success. If you created a game plan to help with the actions you wanted to take you just have to follow them, and follow them consistently.

## SO...WHAT NOW?

If you've got the goals all set and the game plan in place then just keep doing the positive things you're already doing. You can reevaluate the goal and decide if you want to change its direction or what you're working on as you go along. You can pick something else and try to add that into your life as well.

But the consistency of positive habits is what's going to help you get to mastery over your own personal growth.

Just like earning a black belt, the material and the curriculum is right there. You've got to figure it out and practice. You've got to be honest with yourself about the areas you're weak in and work on making them stronger. You may even have others to train with. You're going to make mistakes along the way because the path is hard.

Over time, eventually, somewhere down the road, you get that black belt mastery.

# CHAPTER THREE
# YELLOW BELT

After my friend's death I focused almost solely on my martial arts and teaching. I was in class 4 to 5 times per week and volunteered to help teach classes daily. Every little piece of experience I could get, I wanted. When opportunity came knocking, I was going to be ready.

September 1, 2001 was the very first day I was a "professional martial arts instructor." As in I was actually getting paid to teach. Up to this point I had been a volunteer instructor for several hours a week. It was the first day I stepped into Union UTA martial arts in Union, New Jersey. My instructor's instructor, so let's say my grand instructor, was opening a school and needed someone to assist with running it. I was fortunate enough to be able to get the job.

Union was a world away from where I grew up. Going from the middle of New Jersey farmland to what is basically a suburb of New York City, Union was honestly the most urban town I had ever been to at that point in my life. Admittedly, there was a lot for me to adjust to.

I had assisted in a lot of classes before then and helped other instructors run the school I was originally training at. Other than being in a new environment, this day was no different, my boss took the lead and I assisted throughout the day. There was a lot more I still had to learn, but it was pretty awesome to know that I was on the path that felt right for me, possibly for the first time in my life.

On September 2, 2001 I will never forget the phone call that I got from my new boss.

"Good morning Mr. Nichols, how are you doing today?"

"I'm great sir, thank you. How are you?" I replied.

"I'm doing good thanks." He said." Mr. Nichols, do you have a set of keys to the school?"

"Yes, sir I do."

"OK great, good luck today. I'll check in with you later."

And that was really it. A short call at 9am and I was on my own.

I just got thrown into the deep end of the pool. I had never run a martial arts class by myself. I didn't know how to do an enrollment of a new student. I didn't know how to answer the phone. At that point I don't even think I'd ever mopped a floor by myself. Yet here I was.

In that first year I don't think he came in more than a dozen times. I was forced to learn on my feet. I started studying and learning about business practices, management, and leadership.

Fast forward about 4 1/2 to 5 years of me running a school full-time, six days a week. We'd become the largest school in our organization. When we went to tournaments, we literally brought hundreds of people. I was able to start to develop my own instructor team. After a few twists and turns, I was able to purchase the school and become the owner and chief instructor.

There is a big difference between running a business and not being the owner and being the owner and running the business.  It's almost like being able to play with someone else's money but not have any of the responsibility. At the end of the day, it's still not your business. It's not fully your responsibility. I think I was fortunate that I always treated the school like it was mine. From day one I worked with the mindset that it belonged to me and I would treat it with that respect.  Once I was able to purchase it though, there was a certain amount of uncertainty and weight that came with it. The buck really stopped with me. It was unlike anything I had ever experienced.

Not long after I purchased the school there started to be turmoil within the organization. Some schools within the organization wanted to go in different directions. Different school owners wanted different things for their students. Management wanted things their way. Things were very quickly beginning to fall apart and I had a choice of staying on board with the original owners or branching out on my own. It was an absolutely terrifying experience. It's one thing when you have a group of people making decisions, coming up with ideas, and working together. It's very different when you're the one who gets the absolute final say that could make or break whether or not you're able to cloth and feed your family.

It was my wife, Erica, who ultimately helped me make that decision. We were sitting in the living room of our townhouse one evening while our one-year-old daughter was upstairs asleep. You could imagine the pressure that I was under having just bought a school, not long before having bought a house, and having a child.

I will never forget she said to me, "well do you have an idea on how you would want to do things differently?" I thought about it for a second and said, "well yeah, I've got a ton of ideas. And they're my students so I think I know them best."

She said, "well do you think you can get everything organized enough to do it on your own?"

"Yes," I said.

She looked at me and said, "well then, you've already got your answer. What are you waiting for? Just get organized."

# CHAPTER FOUR

# EARN A BLACK BELT IN ORGANIZATION

It's pretty common sense. When things are organized, things run smoother. Doesn't really matter what you're talking about in this case. Could be the day in day out of your life. Could be organizing your job. Could be organizing your kid's schedules and activities. Whatever it is, having some level of organization is the key to making sure things work in a more functional way.

I will tell you, years ago I was having anxiety and panic attacks. I was at my wits end. I reached a point where handling my business and home life was just not happening. On top of getting the help I needed, I also took this time to get organized. Get myself on a schedule and put systems in place to help me at work and home. It was an absolute game changer for me. You cannot hope to be successful in your career without a certain level of organization. It makes you efficient at getting things done, on timelines, and consistent in your work.

## PLANNING FOR CHAOS

Things come up that we haven't planned for. You get a phone call during the day asking you to switch gears from what you're working on to move to a totally different project. We can prevent these stressors and curveballs from throwing us off. If the majority of the things we're doing are organized, it allows us to change gears to handle things as they come up and then jump right back on task.

There's a big difference between having a general idea of what your work day is going to look like and having certain points planned out. We can't predict everything that's going to happen during our day, but by having an idea of what needs done or what our commitments are, we are much more likely to be able to handle the things that come up.

You cannot be effectively efficient without a certain level of organization. So, the more organized you are, the more efficient you will be. So, if you've got your day planned out, your action items in place, and your time sorted, when chaos pops up, you can handle it! When you aren't very organized and you get thrown a curveball, that's when all hell breaks loose.

# ARM YOURSELF

Think about it simply. Is it easier to try to remember everything you need when you go to the grocery store, or to write it down on a list before you go? Also, there's something to be said about being able to check things off of a list as you accomplish them and the satisfaction that comes with seeing a chore list completely crossed off.

At this point in the history of mankind we don't have any excuse not to be organized. Every single one of us is walking around with a device in our pocket that can pretty much do anything. Your phone is a heck of a lot more useful than just playing click-y games and checking out what's trending. There are plenty of apps, calendars, and ways to set up reminders that we can use to our advantage in organizing our lives. For me, I need two things: a calendar and a task list.

So, I have a couple of different calendars (color coded) that I have to look at for different reasons. I have one calendar that is specifically meant for financial commitments and contractual obligations. Those are set up on a specific day of the week so I don't have to look at it every day. I have another calendar that is just for our family's social events, Doctors appointments, etc. Pretty much anything that affects the whole family. I have a calendar that is just for work events. Things going on in my business then I need to know about on a specific day. Then there is the one that tells me what to do on a daily, weekly, or monthly basis. Which pretty much means if I look at it on Monday it tells me all the chores and things that I should do for every Monday. On the 1st and the 15th of the month it reminds me about billing tasks. You get the idea.

I also take it a step further. If I've got an event coming up on June 1, I will then back track reminders for several weeks or months so I can do any of the work I need for that event over time. If I follow that schedule and stay on it, by the time June 1st rolls around I am well prepared for that day. Stress free and on time.

My task list serves a couple of purposes as well. One is just a brain dump. If I have something popping in my head that I need to do or somebody asks me to do something for them and it's relatively soon, I just throw it on my task list so that when it's time for me to work or even just checking it out in the morning I know what I need to do when it's the right time. Also, all those events that are on my calendar, I transfer them over to my task list on the appropriate days.

So, if I trust in the calendar, move things over to the task list when need be, and just start checking things off, I usually get a large amount of work done. When my task list goes from forty items down to four or five, it's a pretty satisfying feeling.

## AN ASTEROID HITS

OK, so what about when something comes up that needs my immediate attention? No problem.

Handle it the best I can, move anything that I can't do over to the task list to be done, when need be, or move it to the calendar if appropriate. When I'm done dealing with what came up, switch back over to the task list. Unless there are specific, time sensitive items, then when things "come up," you can always go back to your task list after.

It's unrealistic to think that interruptions of unplanned tasks are never going to come up. So, if you are collecting everything you possibly can in your systems, then it's easier to deal with the random items. If you stress out every time something unexpected comes up, it's probably partially because the things you have to do aren't organized properly.

## BRAIN DUMP

Break it down like this. Get things out of your brain and into a trusted system. Then just follow the system. If the system fails, remember, be OK with setbacks, readjust the system and move on. Systems need maintenance every now and then.

It's one of those things that when you have good systems in place then you feel a lot better about making sure you're getting done the things that you need to. It's also about being OK with the things you're not getting done. If they're in a place that you trust and know you will get to at the appropriate time, then you don't have them stressing you out or floating around in your brain. People get stressed because they are trying to not forget anything. So, what do they end up doing? Forgetting something! So, get it out of your brain and into a system.

## LIVING SYSTEM

Just like some of those things we talked about in personal growth, when you start to get organized and set up your systems, it can be a little overwhelming. You're definitely going to need a solid chunk of time to set up those calendars, task lists, and reminders. Once you do that, everything else you do is going to be a lot easier. A couple of years ago I started a master list. The list consists of everything that I do in my business during the year. Setting up testings, ordering belts, setting up tournaments, ordering T-shirts, advertising and marketing, special events for the kids, I mean literally anything. Each item has a sub-list as well. Start with the event date:

- One week before, print paperwork for the event and send out final reminders.
- Two weeks before ordering supplies for the event.
- Three weeks before setting up paperwork.
- Six weeks before, announce the event.

You get the idea.

So, every November I take this list and sit down with my calendar and spend anywhere between 8 to 12 hours planning out the entire next year. Truth is, I dread doing this every year. It takes a ton of time and it's exhausting. However, after I sit down and set everything up, the bulk of the work I need to do for the next year is planned out. I'm always super thankful for the amount of time it saves me for months and months to come. In the long run it saves me countless hours of having to think about what I should be doing, saves me tons of stress, and prevents a lot from falling through the cracks.

No system is foolproof. They need to evolve and change over time. They need to be adjusted. But start with something. Get something in place and adjust it later. But having something in place is going to help get things out of your head and get you working.

## 168 HOURS

Did you know there are 168 hours in a week? I will admit I'm kinda obsessed with this idea. I have so many (so, so many) people that come to me with the time excuse for things. Now I'm not saying that people aren't busy. We all have things going on. But let's say you get perfect sleep. 8 hours a night. Ok that's 56 hours. You work a 40 hour a week job. Let's even take 2 hours a day out for let's say random car travel to and from work or whatever. 10 hours a week for eating. 5 hours a week for general grooming (that seems generous but follow me here). 3 hours a week walking your dog? You've still got 40 hours left. I know my numbers are a little general, but do you see my point? You can't find a way to spare 4 hours a week on fitness? 3 hours building a skill? 2 hours learning something new? It just seems like a lot of time wasted during the week to me.

Where it goes wrong is two main areas. One is not prioritizing your time. If you tell me you want to learn to protect yourself or get in shape but you only want to train once a week, then it's not really a priority, is it? Sorry, that's just the truth. Or watching all 10 hours of that new Netflix show is more important than reading 10 pages of a book per day. You can absolutely do both, go for it. But the book wasn't much of a priority if you didn't set the time aside to do it. So, when we are looking at those task lists and calendars, we need to prioritize what we should/need to do versus what we want to do. What's going to make this happen? Discipline, plain and simple. Yes, sometimes you gotta cheat a little, but for the most part those priorities need to be straight. Are there some legit reasons why you can't do some things? Absolutely. But be careful to make sure your reasons aren't quickly becoming your excuses. There is a big difference between the two.

The second area people go wrong with this is just time management. Looking at your day, week, month, or year and seeing what falls where. Making a plan to be efficient. Getting a few little things done first to get them off your plate and build some momentum. Making sure you've got what you need to do your job so you aren't running around like a maniac in the middle of a project. Making your phone calls at appropriate times so you aren't going, "oh man, I don't have time to do that now." Point is, put things in order so they are done at the right times. That you are setting yourself up for success instead of just getting through those things randomly.

Yes, there is only so much time we have. It's easy for me to break down the hours and tell you what's going on. I know everyone's lives have their own commitments. That's a big part of it though. Commitment. It's not about having time; it's about having the commitment. So, maximize and prioritize your time. If it's important to you, be committed.

## REMEMBER YOUR WHY

Remember "why" you are trying to get organized. Your why is everything. You are trying to efficiently use your time. Time you can use to get work done, spend with your family and friends, to enjoy yourself. Also, you are trying to take pressure off yourself. The more efficient you are with your organization the less stressed you will be. When all those "to do's" are out of your brain then you are going to have more room to come up with new ideas. This is your "why." It's going to make your life easier.

46

Getting organized isn't about making your life so regimented that you can't enjoy yourself. Getting organized is about creating more time for yourself and living just a little more stress-free. Taking a little bit of time to set yourself up for success and get organized has the potential to absolutely change your life. Sit down, take stock, make a plan, put it on your calendar, and go earn that black belt.

# CHAPTER FIVE
# ORANGE BELT

I don't know about you but when I think about the happiest moments of my life, they almost always involve someone else. You spend a lot of time with other people. Your friends, your family, your partner. I would venture to say that almost all of the fun stuff and happy memories that we get out of life involve someone else as well.

The first people you ever start relationships with in life are your parents. We certainly all know that our relationship with our parents can be a roller coaster. There're so many different ways that people can end up growing up with their parents. There are of course several different ways this happens in life. People whose parents may have been absent, married for 50 years and perfectly happy, married for 50 years and completely miserable, one parent passed away, raised by grandparents, and dozens of other variations. I can really only speak on my experience.

In the introduction I mentioned I was a child of divorce. I will say now that the way my life has turned out and the things I've experienced, trust me when I tell you, I would not have changed a thing and could not be happier with where I am in my life and with my relationship to them.

My mother raised me on her own. She is hard-working, determined, often stubborn, and a completely selfless person. She taught me the value of hard work and treating other people fairly. When I was 13 years old, she ended up suffering from four brain aneurysms and lived. It's a medical miracle that she survived. But like I said, she's stubborn. Although the brain aneurysms completely changed her life you would never know that anything ever happened to her. She just takes it as something that happened to her life and continues to live the best she can. She is the complete backbone of our household and I really don't think we could function without her.

Although my parents' marriage did not end well and my father was not around a lot when I was a kid, my mother never said a bad thing about him. She was always respectful of the image that I had in my head as a kid and was very supportive of the times when it was hard for me not having someone around. I will say that I was not always the easiest kid growing up. Especially as a teenager. I know I was very difficult, often argumentative, and definitely not appreciative of the sacrifices that she made for me. Her consistency and love for me is what allowed us to continue to build a strong relationship once I grew up a bit and was more appreciative of what I had in my life.

Fact: my father and I did not have much of a relationship when I was young and even as a teenager. Not even while I was in my 20s or my early 30s. Here is another fact, now we have a stronger relationship than I could've ever imagined. He is an incredible fixture in my life and I am thankful for every moment I get to spend with him.

In 2011 my father was a truck driver. He ended up getting in an accident that left him in a coma and paralyzed from the waist down. I remember going to see him in the hospital when he was in the coma, sitting by his bedside and crying and mentally letting go of any frustration that I had. I really didn't know much about the man lying in that bed. But I knew he was my father. In some ways I was forgiving him and saying goodbye.

He lived through the experience, though it left him wheelchair bound. Over the next five years we talked a small handful of times. I maybe saw him once, the gap between us had grown even further. It was my father-in-law in one of his final acts on this earth that suggested I buy a motorcycle and start riding. Knowing Kurt, I believe he knew it would be the thing that connected me back to my father.

Several months later after Kurt had passed away and I started riding more comfortably I rode to my father's house. Being a lifelong biker, he was not impressed with the little motorcycle that I had, far more preferring if I had a big old Harley. We sat down in his garage which is some type of Mecca of old-school manliness. It's a real motorcycle garage. Anything you could ever need to work on a chopper. To this day, that garage is one of my favorite places to be. At some point during the awkward conversation, not really knowing what to say to each other, we understandably got a little heated.

I don't remember how we got to it, but at one point he said to me "Where have you been in the last five years? I've been stuck in this wheelchair and I needed you."

I quickly replied "Well where were you all those years I needed you?"

He took a deep breath, "Well let's agree that none of that matters and we have now. Let's make the best of that," and we've been inseparable ever since. At this point in my life, I am very happy for the way I grew up. Not getting to know him until the later part of my life has really allowed me a different view on things. I've learned an incredible amount about life and about myself from spending time with him. It's amazing to me how you can be so similar to someone even though you did not grow up together. Every time we sit in that garage, whether it be just the two of us or with friends, turning gears on motorcycles, I feel like a young kid sitting at the grown-up table listening to their adventures and soaking up wisdom. Being able to repair that relationship has been one of the greatest gifts of my life.

If your parents are the first real relationship you end up cultivating in your life, your partner or your spouse is definitely one of the most major ones.

My wife and I have known each other for over 25 years. I would say in that time we've gone through every definition of a relationship that a couple could have. From being friends and minor acquaintances to dating. From breaking up to getting married, to working through difficulties to having an incredibly solid relationship. She likes to say that she "convinced me that marrying her was a good idea." She says it was the best thing she ever did for me. And she is 100% right.

I was immature when we got married. Probably more like a teenager playing house. I think we both say the reason why we get along so well now is because we went through all of our difficulties in the beginning of our marriage. It was really just poor communication and not understanding how to compromise. Mostly me. I think the best thing that ever happened to us was our early frustrations. We grew and changed as we've been together and as we got older. The advantage is we really like who we are both growing into.

We've been married now for more than 15 years and other than being an amazing partner, a great friend, and an unbelievable support system, she's also an incredible mother. Parenting is a relationship on a totally different level. So just a heads up, that's going to get covered in a chapter later.

# CHAPTER SIX

# EARN A BLACK BELT IN RELATIONSHIPS

To really "earn" a black belt in relationships we have to realize the physical, emotional, and mental commitment it takes to cultivate these relationships over long periods of time. We interact with so many different types of people and have different relationships on many different levels. We have family that we may or may not be close to, our partners and spouses, close friends, friends that we still feel connected to even though we haven't spoken to them in ages, acquaintances, work colleagues, and people that we just have to interact with on a daily basis. Different things have to go into each of these types of relationships. At the same time, they also have some key factors that make them all similar.

## CONSISTENCY AND RELIABILITY

If you care for someone, they need to be able to rely on you. Within reason of course. If you want to know if someone would have your back at 3 o'clock in the morning then you need to be willing to do the same thing for them. This list of people might be very short in your life or it might be very long. That's really dependent on the relationships you've cultivated and your personal character. It doesn't even have to be the big things, but the little things add up as well. Within my close circle of friends and family there is never a phone call or text message that does not go returned rather quickly. Consistent communication among the people you care about shows them that they are important and that you care. If they aren't the same type of person, you've got to be the one to accept that, or decide if you can't. Not all your friends are going to have the same habits and personality that you do. But this is about you, working on your relationships. You can't control what they do, but you can choose how you want to interact with them.

Part of the way people choose their friends is based on that person's behaviors. Over time you're showing a set of behaviors to people that lead them to decide if you're the type of person they wanna be around. If your behaviors are consistent and in line with their morals and values then you end up friends. As soon as you demonstrate a behavior outside of your normal set, it can send up a red flag. This could be for a completely acceptable reason that a friendship can withstand. Accidents happen and friendships can be repaired, but consistency of your behaviors and your attitude really send a signal to others. If your behavior and actions are inconsistent, don't be surprised if that friendship fades away. People do grow apart for various reasons, it could be time, space, or a variety of factors that have nothing to do with you as a person. But it could also be something due to your actions over a given time.

It's not that hard. How you act will directly affect the relationships you have. This isn't a surprise to anyone. But I do challenge you to look at your relationships. Make a list of the last 10 people you interacted with. Friends, your spouse, work colleagues, a person at the supermarket. What did you present to them? How did you act? Yes, sure, maybe you were having a good day so everything felt great. Then look at a few while you were having a bad day. When you were stressed and under pressure. How were all those interactions then. I believe that even the random people we interact with deserve a certain level of respect. Just because we don't know them doesn't mean we shouldn't treat them with decency. If they were our friends and our inner circle, how are we treating them? Are we taking them for granted? Even our friendships and close relationships take work.

Though people you work with or clients that you have to interact with may not be your friends, showing them a certain level of consistency in your behaviors does build trust. Building that trust nurtures the business relationship. Your reliability at work also builds trust with your co-workers. If you are consistently meeting deadlines and customer expectations then that relationship is going to lead to more business. Someone who is consistently dropping the ball and breaking promises isn't going to make it very far in business. So those relationships with the people we work with or the people we work for are incredibly important to our livelihood. So, although these people might not be our spouse, our family, or our close friends, we sometimes need to put in even more effort.

## TRUST

So, what are you doing to build trust in the relationships around you? Again, being consistent in your actions and reliable to people does build trust. Be a person of your word. If you tell someone you're going to do something, do it. If you fall short or the plans change, take accountability as soon as possible. Sometimes falling short of something and taking accountability for it openly and honestly builds more trust than actually achieving the goal. (Don't mess things up on purpose) Owning up to your word one way or another shows people around you that you have integrity. A person with great integrity is a person that's easy to trust. You can still have integrity when falling short. Don't mistake these two things.

Even when it comes to business there's been times where I've fallen short of a mark. Where for whatever reason a promise I had made didn't end up working out. Or something had to change from what I had originally said. This is just the nature of life. You can't predict everything. I'm open and honest. I'm open about if something changed, why it changed or why I fell short. I take accountability for it and let people know what I'm going to do to make it right. It's a lot easier and builds a more positive relationship than just throwing my hands up in the air and saying "well it changed and that's just the way it is." We are human! Taking accountability reminds others of this sometimes. As long as it's not an every time thing, then it's ok. But be humble and honest.

For the people that are close to you, to build trust in that relationship, be vulnerable. Don't be afraid to confide in other people. There's nothing wrong with being vulnerable and discussing your feelings with people that are your friends or family. Confiding in others when you have a problem is not putting a burden on that person. They can choose what they want to do with that information. If they really are someone of quality, then it's actually going to end up making the relationship stronger. Vulnerability should not be seen as a negative. We can't be expected to handle every single event in our life, every emotion, every reaction, completely perfect. Everybody takes their lumps sometimes. So being vulnerable to the people that are closest to us shows them that we trust them as well. It also leaves the door open in the future for them to be more open with you. Being vulnerable in the right situation can end up being a strength, not a weakness. Maybe that person has incredible advice on how to help the situation, or maybe they're just a good shoulder to lean on. It should never be looked down upon and is absolutely a way to build trust. If I never opened up to my wife and was not vulnerable with her about some of the fears and doubts that I've had in my life, we would not be where we are today. If I never gave her the opportunity to hear the things that stressed me out or that I wasn't sure about then there would've been an incredible amount of input that I would've missed out on. Also, we never would've built trust or openness in our relationship which could lead to negativity and emotional distress, damaging our marriage. Don't be afraid to share!

Communication as well! People want to know what's going on. Even if they are an easy person that has a "go with the flow" attitude, you still have to communicate with them. Your spouse, friends, and clients all want to be in the know. Taking a little extra time to communicate ideas, changes, and plans can go a long way. This seems like common sense but it's about not being in the "I can do it better myself" attitude that we can easily fall into. If whatever you have going on involves another person, communicate. Even if we have already resolved or moved forward, what does it hurt to communicate more often?

Another part of communication that is a skill in itself is being a good listener. If you are talking to a person whose relationship you value then make sure they know you are listening when they speak. Ask them questions about when you are discussing. Hear the answers. Don't listen to them, hear them. When you ask that question, be sincere. You should really want to know the answer and let them give it. The more you are showing them you are engaged in the conversation the more they are going to want to have it with you. This benefits you regardless of who you are speaking to.

I have a friend that I've known for many, many years. He's a few years older than me and from the first day I met him and even 20 years later, I have always admired that when he asks you a question, you really believe that he wants to know the answer. I enjoy conversations with him because they have a certain quality to them. I feel listened to and engaged with. I make an effort to use this skill in my own conversations with people. He's better at it than me, admittedly. But I know my trying to copy this behavior makes the conversations I have with others more valuable.

## EFFORT AND EXPERIENCES

For any type of relationship to be successful you have to be an active participant. You have to put in the effort. You've got to put effort into your marriage. You've got to put effort into staying close with your family, especially when you no longer live together. You've got to put effort into your friendships. And you've got to put effort into building relationships with coworkers and clients. An extra phone call or a text message once a week can go a long way to let someone know that you're thinking of them. Checking in or being the one to try to make plans show someone that you care.

Staying connected with today's modern technology should make things pretty easy. I've got a couple of different group chats online and I use to stay connected with groups of friends. I use my calendar to set the reminders to reach out to certain people. On my personal daily task list it reminds me to try to create a nice moment with my wife daily. Whether that is making the effort to make sure she knows she's loved or for the two of us just trying to share a laugh and have some fun. I have a reminder to have a good moment with my daughter daily. Especially as she's getting older and doing more of her own things, I want to make sure she still feels connected so she knows I am there if she needs me.

So, make the effort. Make the phone call to the friend you haven't talked to in a long time. Send out the text messages, contact them through social media. Whatever it is, make the effort to show someone you care about them. When you make the effort, it shows that other person that they're important to you and that strengthens the relationship.

Make the effort at work. Have you ever read a book on interacting with people or talking to people? Have you ever put in the time and effort to educate yourself on dealing with others? The people we work with or the clients we have may not have the same relationship with us as our friends do, but learning how to interact with them positively still builds that relationship. Like I said earlier, building a relationship builds trust. There is a ton of information out there about customer service, body language, and having positive interactions with clients. If you work in a job that has you interacting with a lot of people, do yourself a favor and learn these skills.

## COMMON SENSE

The majority of this chapter is frankly common sense. But how many of us actually take the time to put in the extra steps to really cultivate these relationships? With our parents, our family, close friends, our spouses, our extended friends, our coworkers, or with our clients. Although each of these areas may have different levels of importance in our life, the way that we handle each one is really very similar. Treat these people with respect. Show them that you care. Have clear communication. Be true to your word. Be open and honest. Can't those things be said about every single relationship we have in our life? Earning a black belt in relationships really shouldn't be that hard. We just need to make the decision that we are going to invest in others. The reward is then, that others learn they can invest themselves in us.

This should be an easy one. No, I do not know your specific situation. I recognize that several factors can make this chapter much harder than it sounds. Trauma we may have experienced, anxieties, or a variety of factors affect our relationships in many ways. So as much as I am doling out general information, your specific situation may require a deeper dive. So, I encourage you to take it.

So, let's keep your work relationships with clients or coworkers simple here. You've got a job; you know the people you interact with there and you know you have to meet certain standards. I would encourage you as I know the more personable you make yourself the more of a pleasure you are going to be to work with or have repeat clients from. I'm not saying be a pushover, I said be personable. Make the effort to be a little more outgoing. Smile, talk a little. It's not a lot.

Also remember the fact that you may honestly not like every person you have to interact with. It's easy to decide you just don't like someone and don't want to be their friend, but it's not so easy when you are talking about your work. You frankly may not like all your co-workers or clients. That doesn't mean you can't still be personable and workable with them. All the things we've discussed still apply. You still have to develop a relationship with them so the job is being done effectively or so the clients are still happy. Patience is the key here. You can't let your negative feelings come through; you've still got to be professional.

If you have difficulties with your friends and family relationships you need a deep dive on why. Are these relationships worth keeping? Sometimes they aren't able to be repaired. Rarely is the anger and animosity we hold onto worth keeping though. If it's just a matter of not being as close to people as you would like, then just try. You won't know until you do. Relationships ebb and flow. Everyone is living their own lives. Growing apart isn't always personal.

Keep dating your partner. You live with them; you're building a life with them. You are so invested in being with this person that you have to keep some things in perspective. Keep having fun with them. Be open with them. When things are hard, be honest about it. No, there is no guarantee that these relationships work out. Not at all. But don't let it be for lack of trying. No, the person you married may not be the person you are with years later. People change. Hopefully as you both change and grow you do so together. By encouragement, communication, humility, and intimacy. It takes work. Like everything else. It takes work. Make it worth it.

# CHAPTER SEVEN
## GREEN BELT

We are continually faced with new challenges throughout life. For my wife, Erica, and I, we had been married for a few months. We were living in a small apartment and working hard. I was running the school but didn't own it yet. We were faced with a drastic challenge. In 2006 there was a writer's strike. Television came to a screeching halt. What was a newly married couple supposed to do with their time?

So, there we were, my wife and I sitting with friends to dinner one evening. Since I worked evenings, we went out with friend's a lot after I got out. The waiter, who happened to be the son of one of the friends we were there with, brought a high chair up to the table and sat it down between my wife and I.

"Hey man, you're going to need this," he said.

"What are you talking about bro?" I replied. He smiled and said, "No man, you're really going to need this. "

As I looked around at the rest of the table, which were all smiles and staring at me, my wife handed me the pregnancy test. Being the stupid 27-year-old that I was, not wanting to show any emotion, I played dumb. My wife will still swear that I didn't know what was going on, but I did. I hid my shock well, but I got it right away. Later that evening, when no one else was around, I let my emotions show. We sat in the car and I remember bawling my eyes out. Everything had changed.

Like all first-time parents the next few months were both exciting and filled with anxiety. We did everything we could to prepare our home and our lives.

Fast forward several months to the day my daughter was born. The day before Father's Day. After a grueling 38-hour labor, my daughter had come into this world. A half an hour after she was born my wife and I had decided on a name. I snuck out into the hallway and called the company that handles our black belts for the school. I ordered an embroidered belt with her name on it, with the hopes that one day that she would claim it.

I remember the day we left the hospital. Putting her in her car seat and placing her in the back seat of the car. We both got in the front and closed our car doors and looked at each other. Taking a sign, we both started to laugh. I don't think I ever drove so carefully home in my entire lifetime.

Throughout the years that followed I can't say that Alexa trained very often. It wasn't really her fault, we lived almost an hour away from the school. Training at home had proven itself to just be an activity in playtime. She came to class every now and then and enjoyed throwing a few punches and kicks playing around with Dad, but she wasn't the type of kid ever that took things too seriously.

At the beginning of the summer of her fifth-grade year of school we had a discussion about what she wanted to do that summer. Typically, she had done little summer camps, playdates, and all usual summer activities.

"Alexa, do you want to go to a summer camp or something like that this year?"

"No dad, I'm going to go to work with you every day," she said.

Very suspiciously and with a bit of an eyebrow raise, I responded, "really?" in my mind thinking okay, let's see how long this lasts.

That first summer she ended up pretty much working a full-time job, training and teaching martial arts 5 to 6 days a week. This continued every summer since, as well as every day off school, every vacation, and sometimes even evenings after a long drive in.

When she tested for her black belt, I knew that I am very fortunate that the image I had in my head of this little girl growing up and earning her black belt ended up coming true. I never forced her to train and I always gave her the option to try other activities, but wrapping that belt around her waist felt like I had succeeded as a parent. And although she still had a long way to go in life, I feel like I can check that one off of my list.

I have only experienced a few stages of life with my daughter, I do know that I've learned a great deal about myself because of her. I've set goals that I never would've set, readjusted goals to achieve more, developed personal relationships with people that I never would have. I've gone to places and done great things because of her. I've also looked at myself as a person and have made adjustments and grown to try to be a better parent. To me, this may be the most important job I will ever have.

# CHAPTER EIGHT

# EARN A BLACK BELT IN PARENTING

If you have a child then this should be one of the top things you attempt to earn a black belt in. Parenting. If you have a child, then you know for a fact it's also one of the most difficult ones. Being a parent is one of the most rewarding and most difficult things we can do in our lives. It's never ending, always changing, has highs and lows, and there really aren't any breaks. Beyond just trying to keep kids alive and healthy, we are tasked with teaching them the mass majority of what they know about life. Even the things they don't learn from us, we've taught them how to receive and respond to that information. There are literally millions of things that we could do to screw our kids up.

No pressure.

Man, raising a kid can be hard! And frustrating, and tiring, and expensive. And completely worth it. When you put in the work. My opinion, I just don't understand people that don't want to put the work into their kids. Sorry. Just how I feel. Because for all the Hard stuff that happens there are a million amazing things that happen.

We can also take pride in their successes as they continue to grow. Never forget, as they grow up, so are we. Life is much different now from when we were kids. Depending on how old you are, that is true several times over. The way that we learned, were taught, Interacted, and were raised is completely different to how things are now. In many of our cases the internet didn't even exist. Now the world can't function without it. Also, every kid is different. People with multiple children will talk about how completely different each of their kids' personalities are, and that dealing with them has to be done differently. So, realize that anything that I give you my opinion on, might be different in your situation. But at least I can give you an opinion or an idea that you can then adjust. I can't tell you how to raise your kid, in fact it's one of those subjects I really try not to tell people how to do at all. But I can at least tell you a couple of things that I've done with my kid, that I feel like were good decisions and it turned out well.

## BABIES

Get in the fight. Change diapers, change their clothes, feed them, make a schedule for who sleeps and who gets up with the kid. Play with your kid. Play with them a lot. Interaction is a really big deal. Be active and involved. Everybody says that kids don't come with an instruction manual, but that's just not true. There're so many books out there on parenting and dealing with babies. Also, if you know anybody who's ever done it, get as much advice as you can and figure out what works for you. So, when you say you don't know what to do, you're just being lazy. You can learn. You owe it to that kid.

Just do everything you can not to be a hands-off parent. Not only is it going to strengthen your relationship and bond with your child, but it's also going to improve your relationship with your partner. Nobody wants to feel like they're alone when they're completely exhausted and learning to deal with the baby. .

Yes, this is going to be hard. If it's your first it's going to be an incredibly big change to your life. Step up into this change. Don't shy away from it. This isn't a house plant. This is a human being you are now going to be responsible for, so do it to the best of your ability.

## YOUNG TODDLER

When I think of a young toddler, I think of a kid that developed the ability to walk and crawl but really can't communicate well yet. Or at least just like when they were a baby, screaming and yelling is really their primary means of communication. You can't get mad about that. It's not their fault they can't communicate. So, when they are screaming and hollering don't make them feel ashamed or bad about it. I get we all get frustrated, but next time you hear someone yell at a baby or a toddler stop and think. The kid couldn't exactly give a major explanation of why they did the exact opposite of what they were told. Most likely they didn't have the understanding or emotional stability either.

This is also a great time to start to build their confidence. Let them explore, let them do things. Let them get into things. Safety minded of course, but it's OK to let them walk out in front, be a few feet ahead of you and roaming around in the right situation. Don't shy away from every little thing. You don't want them to fear the world. You want them to build confidence in exploring and trying new things.

Going to say it again. Play with your kid. In fact, roughhouse with your kid a little bit too. Boy or girl doesn't matter, start roughhousing with them a little bit now. You're going to be thankful later when your kid isn't fragile.

# OLDER TODDLER/YOUNG KID

Once a kid can move and communicate, forget about it, you're dealing with a totally different human being. Now they can really come into their own personality and have opinions on things and wants and desires. This is why it really gets hard when their thoughts and opinions are not in line with yours. Don't embarrass your kid and discipline them too much in public. Even though they're a kid, let them keep their dignity. Anytime we went anywhere or were going to experience a new situation, we would try to pre-frame our daughter. Talk about what was gonna happen and what the expectation of behavior was. If something goes wrong, of course you have to deal with it at that moment, just make sure that your response is equal to the situation and not overblown. Later on when your child is in their "safe space" and things are calm, have a conversation. Ask a lot of questions. As an instructor who's been dealing with kids for well over 20 years, the biggest piece of advice I can tell people is to ask kids questions. When you ask a child a question, you force their brain to work differently and stop to answer it as opposed to just hearing the information you're saying. They're more likely to learn from this. Especially as they get older, stopping to answer that question is going to have an impact on them.

Continue to build that confidence. Let them lead when you go out in the world, if the situation is right. If you're walking in a crowded area keeping them by your side is best, but there's got to be times where you let them take the point. Also, let them do the talking. When you go to a restaurant or order something, let them talk for themselves. It's going to get them used to having to speak to people they're intimidated by. It also lets them speak to a stranger in a safe environment. If you're at a park or in a playgroup, have them go make friends on their own. Insist that they interact with other kids. Teaching your kid to get out in their world and use their voice is huge. Doing it at home is one thing, this is their safe space that they're in control of, doing it in other places is going to be a massive help to them as they get older.

I think it's great to involve kids in your passions and the things you like to do. I also think it's important to be mindful that they might not be interested in those things and want to do their own stuff. My daughter must've tried at least 8 to 10 different activities as she was growing up. Different types of musical instruments, different types of sports, dance, gymnastics, you get the picture. She did martial arts off and on with me for several years, but I never really pushed the issue of her being more consistent. I'm just fortunate that she came to that in her own time and became passionate about it on her own. Maybe there's a little bit of reverse psychology in there, who knows. But the point is, letting them try some different activities is healthy. Kids are guided by their excitement and their emotion and even something that they've liked doing for several years can change very quickly. We always had a rule where any activity Alexa was involved in, she had to either finish the season, or the session before she was allowed to move on. She also was expected to verbally explain why she wanted to move on. This way, we could try to avoid the normal kid's answer of, "I don't like it." By getting her to have to verbalize it a little more seemed to always keep her in touch with her feelings about the situation.

I've always been a big talker, so I definitely feel like spending a good amount of time interacting and talking with your kid is very important. Given the right situation or moment, having long conversations with your kid can really be educational for both of you. There's definitely a difference between a conversation and a lecture. A mistake that I admittedly make many, many times. But taking the time to have conversations, explain things, and get feedback can really go a long way. As I said before, ask questions. Especially as children continue to get older, questions become more thought-provoking for them. It puts them in a position to have to verbalize their answers in a bit more detail than just a yes or a no.

## GETTING OLDER

As kids continue to get older there's a time period where they are completely controlled by their emotions. Emotions which ebb and flow and change quickly. Which pretty much means nobody's in charge.

Be patient. The frustrations of one moment may not last very long. But the patience you have with them can be a lot. Trust me, I very often need to take my own advice as I am completely known for being a person that gets frustrated and stressed very easily. I think it's important that we as parents have to be open to the idea that we make mistakes too. There've been plenty of situations I've handled, and then afterwards, felt bad about how it went. At least for me, when I feel I've been too strict or overreacted to a situation, I go and talk to her about it. Parents make mistakes too and I don't think there's anything wrong with your kid knowing that.

Try to think back to your experiences growing up. All the different emotional, social, and educational landmines you dealt with. It's easy to look back and make judgments, but when your kid is going through it there's going to be differences.

## SCHOOL

So, if we are talking about them getting older then we should also mention school. All I can say is never forget that you are your child's biggest advocate. Since you aren't going to be with your child all day long then you aren't going to get the play by play of how every day goes. So, when things aren't clear or seem off, step in. Not every education model is right for every kid. Every kid learns differently. I know kids have to learn to adjust to the system, but it's up to us to make sure the system is adjusting to our kids as much as they can too.

My kid started pre-K, kindergarten, and 1st grade like most other kids, public school. From day 1 something seemed a bit off. She was a square peg we were trying to put into a round hole. She was always a social and confident kid. But in school it was a lot of "sit down and be quiet." Yes of course, this is necessary and needs to be taught to kids. But something was just off.

We went through the whole process of talking to the school and looking for help, but the options and answers we were receiving just didn't help our situation.

On the advice of a friend, we went to a Mayfair at another school nearby. If you don't know what a Mayfair is, picture a huge pole with ribbons dangling from it, tons of flowers, kids dancing everywhere. If I'm totally honest. I laughed about it for weeks. The whole thing was just silly to me. Such a completely different school activity then anything I had ever experienced and at that time, ridiculous to me. But a few weeks later after some more research and many family conversations, it really became, just because it "wasn't like that '' for either my wife or I growing up, doesn't mean it can't be like that for our daughter. Long story short, finding an alternative education school helped her to excel moving forward. Although it wasn't the way I grew up, it doesn't mean it wasn't for her. We had to advocate for her and put in the work to get her the education she deserved.

I would also add this. And yes, every family is different. I was not from a household that expected straight A's in school. Honestly, passing was enough. I know kids face a lot of pressure today when it comes to grades. We have been very fortunate in our household with our expectations in this area. And it's simply this. Your best effort is expected. Whatever your grade, if you can tell me that you truly tried your best, that's all I can ask. And it's served us very well so far. Because on the times (rare times) her grades aren't great, asking if she really tried her best has been a good learning experience, and has prompted improvement afterwards.

## MOST IMPORTANT JOB YOU'VE EVER HAD

There's so much we have learned from our parents. Even if you had a difficult situation and you didn't have your parents growing up, then you hopefully learned that you want to be there for your kids. If you're like me, a child of divorce, then there are a totally different set of lessons you may or may not want them to learn. If part of the point of being a parent is to give our kids opportunities we didn't have, and to learn things we didn't, then we have a lot of work to do. That work isn't always going to be easy, and it's certainly going to test us. But that's your kid, and that's a special relationship.

I know I sound super old when I say this, but there's a lot of things my kid does nowadays that I just don't understand. Think back to when we were kids, and we now know our parents must have often felt the same way. Maybe I have this opinion because I work with kids, teenagers and adults, but I do believe that you have to accept that it's a different world. You can teach good values and lessons to your children, but the way that they learn certain things is going to be different than the way you did. So, the way you communicate with them may be very different from the way your parents communicated with you. Or even the way that you have to discipline them or teach them. Point is, be open about it. It's a different world that we grew up in than our kids are growing up in. The only thing we can do is teach them the best we can and create a secure environment where they know we are there for them if they need us. Let them be who they are. Help them to be better than who we are.

# CHAPTER NINE

# BLUE BELT

After having been with the same martial arts organization for about 10 years, things fell apart. The organization was going through some issues with management and it was clear that it was time to separate from them. Breaking away and going out on my own was terrifying. There was a certain comfort and safety that came with being in the organization. You teach what they told you to teach, participate in the events they told you to do, and basically run things the way they told you to run them. Being out on my own I had a completely different sense of responsibility and pressure. Even more so than just owning the school.

There's a lot of power in being the person that makes every single decision. There's also a lot of doubt and pressure. I was suddenly in a world where if I decided to change something and I was wrong, it could lead to financial hardship or even ruin. If I was right, it could lead to continued growth.

All these years later there are even still times where I hesitate to change something with the reason of, "well that's just how it's always been done." You can actually forget you are the boss and can change what you want. It's actually very liberating at times when you remember.

Being away from the safety of the organization also meant that I had to learn things about marketing, different office management systems, class and event planning, and a completely different level of customer service. I had to up my business IQ fast. For someone who barely graduated high school, took 5 years to get my 2-year degree, and was not an avid reader, this was a big task.

I stayed on my own for over several years. I had many opportunities to join other organizations, but after the negative experience I had previously, I didn't want to join an organization where someone else was telling me what to do. Once you get used to making your own decisions and putting trust in yourself it's hard to go back. In fairness, after a few years I got smart and did not make all the decisions on my own. I began to bring all important matters to our senior staff and put everything up for a vote. Since I'm not the only person on the floor teaching, I'm not the only person that should be making decisions. I might get the final say, but hearing from the collective group of people in charge has been incredibly helpful.

Sometime during 2016 I will completely admit to being burnt out. I was just exhausted all the time and had lost a lot of my motivation. One afternoon I was scrolling through the Internet looking for some teaching inspiration. YouTube directed me to a video of a man teaching dirty boxing and knife combat. SAMI combat systems would become an addiction for me. I fell in love with the material fast. I even sent an email to their headquarters thanking them for putting the material online because I found some inspiration in it. The gentleman who ran the school, Peter Weckauf, sent me a simple email back saying thank you he appreciated my kind words. The organization's headquarters was in Austria, and a few months later they posted that they were looking to come to America for the first time to teach. A few emails, a few FaceTime conferences, and some organizing later and the rest was history.

Many of the people I've met through SAMICS have become some of the best friends I've ever had. Joining the organization has done nothing but benefit my program and myself. It's been a perfect balance of following an organization's rules while still having a great deal of control as well. I've been fortunate enough to be able to fly to Europe several times and experience things I never thought I would in my lifetime. Also, as a teacher, it has allowed me to continue my own education while still being able to teach others and grow my business.

When I was younger, I had a friend who asked me what I did for a living. I told him I was a martial arts instructor. He told me I was wrong. That I wasn't a martial arts instructor, but I was a business owner. I remember arguing with him at the time. That he was wrong and teaching was always going to be my main focus.

After years of hands-on education running my business. I now often hear my friends' words coming out of my mouth when I work with consulting clients. Being a teacher is only one of the hats that I wear in my business. Yes, I am still a martial arts instructor, but I'm also about a hundred other things that add up to business owner.

## CHAPTER TEN
# EARN A BLACK BELT IN BUSINESS

I am by far no expert in business. I know my profession well, but honestly, there are plenty of times when I'm hanging out with a group of friends and as some chat about their profession, I'm just completely left in the dark. I know that I'm really good at what I do. Having run my business now for over 20 years, I think what makes me an "expert" is that if there's been a mistake to make, trust me, I've made it and I've learned from it. So, when we talk about earning a black belt in business for me it's really just based on mindset.

Whether you work for someone else in a company or work for yourself owning a business, the things we're going to talk about have you covered. Ideas that can lead you towards success in business are the same for both. If you work for yourself, applying the right mindset will lead to the growth and consistency of your business. If you're working for someone else, applying the right mindset will make you an even more valuable employee and possibly help you rise through the ranks.

# CONSISTENCY

You probably know this already, consistency is key. Whatever job you have, whatever thing you do, consistently do it right. Do it on time, do it with quality, do it with care, do it consistently. Consistency in your work proves that you can handle the work. It shows that you care about the work, builds trust and reliability. Show up on time, show up every time. Have a certain standard of quality in anything you do and always follow through with it.

If I was consistently starting my classes late then I'm showing the parents that I don't respect their time. I'm showing them that the rules that I've set forth have no meaning, and I'm really showing them that they're not important to me. I'm very particular about making sure our classes run on time every time. On the occasions we end up running one class into another and needing to be a moment or two late, trust me, we hustle to get back on track. The consistency of showing the parents that we run on a tight schedule also helps them with their planning. They are more likely to adjust their schedules to be on time and respect our rules. That also teaches the children the importance of being on time and properly prepared beforehand. So, my consistent habit doesn't just help me, it helps everyone else as well.

If I had an employee that was consistently doing a great job, finishing their work properly and in a timely manner, I'm more likely to want to give them more responsibility and value them. When you're valued at your job because of your hard work and focus you're much more likely to end up making more money in the long run and enjoying your time there.

There's also something to be said about growth in consistency. If I'm consistently doing my tasks correctly, I will get more efficient at them, and eventually be able to evolve them. So, whatever it is that you're doing, make sure that it's right and make sure that it's consistent. It's about that hustle. If we are talking about business, we are talking about work and work ethic. That is reflected in your consistency. Your work ethic is going to define your career. Your drive, your willingness, your adaptability, are all going to be factors that decide where you land. So being consistent in your work is going to pay off.

## BE A PROBLEM SOLVER

Regardless of where you're working, from one point of view your job is to solve problems. If you're in the restaurant industry you're solving someone's problem of being hungry. You're solving someone's problem of needing a place to go on date night. And when you can solve someone else's problems and you've done your job, then they're appreciative of it. If you're the person creating problems by not doing your job properly, you're much less likely to have repeat business or rise through the ranks.

But be a problem solver. Customer service is one of the key factors of running a good business. If you work at a job where you have to interact with the public, constantly figuring out ways to solve one of their problems, it's going to be one of the things that makes you rise to the top. If you're in a situation where you can't solve their problem, at least try to do something to make them still feel positive. Give them something a little extra, follow up with them, give something to at least soften the blow. Be that problem solver.

If you don't interact with the public at all but you still have fellow employees you have to interact with, be their problem solver. Be the person that brings solutions to the table instead of the person that brings problems. Or if you have to bring a problem, make sure that you've got ideas on how to fix it as well. Showing up with just a problem and no solution brings down the entire group. At least by having some ideas or forethought shows others that you're making the effort.

If you own a business, you are problem solving on a daily basis. So, adopt the mindset. When issues come up you can see them as problems or opportunities. We have had many situations where we have made major changes to our program based on a problem a client has brought us. Since I have to deal with so many similar clients (families with kids or adults) when someone brings me a problem, I assume it might be an issue for others. So, it's at least worth looking at and seeing if changes or improvements can be made.

## COMMUNICATION

Many of our jobs and careers involve interacting with other people. That doesn't even have to be in person, it could be via email, phone, text, the Internet. Whatever it is, you've still got to be a communicator. There can be a huge difference between communicating with your boss, communicating with your peers, communicating with your subordinates, your clients, and even the general public that you might need to interact with. Knowing how to communicate and doing it correctly is key.

Having a clear chain of communication for any situation can help to solve many problems, as well as create customer loyalty, or employee reliability. If you're working on a project at work with some of your peers, communicating properly about that project, each other's responsibilities, deadlines, and anything that might else come up with the project is huge. Other people are also relying on you for information. Why not go the extra step and create specific times you're going to touch base, email each other updates, do anything you have to do to make sure that everyone is clear on what they need to get done for the project to be completed.

When we have things we need to communicate at my martial arts school, we try to do it through multiple channels to make sure that we're hitting everyone. Everything goes on our website, goes in our weekly emails, goes on our information board, gets announced in class, and very often also has handouts going home. Making sure that the information that my clients need is available in a timely manner and through several channels to make sure it's working for everyone.

It's also not just making sure you're communicating consistently but also making sure that you're communicating properly. How are you when talking to other people? Do you feel like you clearly explain things? Are you receptive to hearing things back from them? Do you get defensive easily? Not just in your words but in your body language. I've always made an effort when speaking with clients or my staff to try to be upbeat and enthusiastic. I want people to feel positive when they speak with me and even feed off some of that energy. It helps make sure other people are feeling good about the program and what they are doing. Of course, if we're dealing with a more serious situation or a problem I dial it back, making sure that I'm calm, focused, and respectful. Learning to read the energy of the other person and work with it can really go a long way.

A massive part of communicating isn't what you say or how you say it, but just your ability to listen. People want to be heard, and sometimes the best thing to do is let them say everything that they want to say. Always be an active listener, focused on the other person and commenting when appropriate, but still letting them finish speaking is huge. It's all too often that people aren't necessarily listening but waiting for their turn to speak, or even creating their own turn (interrupting). This doesn't always lead to a positive experience when communicating. When that person is done and they've gotten their thoughts and words out, mirror it back to them. Make sure they know that you understand what they're talking about. Even if you disagree. You can't force someone to see something different when they have their mind set on something. It's kind of like being a problem solver, you're not going to solve their problem by proving them wrong, you're only creating more frustration. I always like to go back to the old feel, felt, found method.

"I understand how you feel, I've felt the same way before, what I found is."

Anyone who spent time learning to communicate and deal with people has probably heard a version of this method. But it's important because it shows the other person that you've heard what they've said, that you empathize in some way or have experienced it with others, and you've found certain types of results. If you're going to disagree, this is one of the best ways to do it.

## EDUCATION

Regardless of your field of expertise, working on your own as an entrepreneur, as a boss with employees of your own, or working for someone else, there are still plenty of ways to expand your education.

This is something I just can't stress enough.

I will admit that when I was a teenager and into college, I did not take my education seriously. I've been left with lots of gaps in my learning and a great many things that I don't know about that I probably should. I did get lucky enough to develop a passion for reading when I was in my late 20s. All thanks to a Star Wars novel that I picked up in the airport while my wife and I were going on vacation. What started out as reading a ton of fiction books then developed into reading educational books, motivational, and developmental books as well.

There are plenty of different ways that you can educate yourself about your field or job that you work in. Whether you're using audiobooks, reading, taking classes online, watching YouTube videos, or anything of the sort, the more knowledge you gain the better off you're going to be.

Don't always think what you're educating yourself about has to be in regards to your particular field. You can also be studying books on leadership, communication, or learning to interact with other people. Teaching yourself to be a better leader and communicator can help in so many different fields and careers. If you're an educator, why not read a book in learning to read body language and nonverbal communication. If you're a manager at a company why not read a book on leadership and working with others. If you're a law-enforcement officer why not learn more about communication. These are all things that can help us tremendously by association.

The world around us is constantly changing. If we want to stay relevant in our careers, we might need to learn things about social media or marketing, or different types of computer software used online. There are plenty of things in my career that I didn't have to know about 5 or 10 years ago, that now if I want to stay relevant, I at least have to have a decent handle on. If you stay stagnant in your knowledge, that knowledge is only going to be usable for so long. Continually working to educate yourself on new things can have benefits that will extend your career.

Have you thought about hiring a coach? There are a variety of coaches out there to help with tons of different areas. You've got marketing coaches, motivational coaches, leadership coaches, and general business consultants. Regardless of who you are, there are always going to be people out there who know more or who know the areas you don't.

Do you have a friend or friend's that you talk business with? That motivates you when it comes to your work. I have a small group of friends that I speak to weekly. Some are business owners and some are not. But they are a group of motivated people, enthusiastic and of a similar mindset to me. We touch base weekly just to check in. Update each other on our projects and work. We motivate and inspire each other. We talk about the books we are reading and how we are educating ourselves. In some ways it's like having a coach; someone who will help to push you and even give you ideas from time to time. Find that person in your life that is like minded. Even if you don't directly work together, you can still support each other.

## FILL THE GAPS

You can't do everything all the time. Even with education you can't be expected to know everything. There are just certain aspects of our jobs that would take too much expertise to be done effectively, and we just might not have the time to do it right.

Sure, if I needed a new website, I'm sure there are classes online that would teach me how to do it and I could try to put something together. But it's going to come out much better if I have an expert do it for me.

Sometimes expanding our network of people that we can work and interact with is a better option than trying to do everything ourselves. Projects can come out more professional and deadlines can be met easier with a little help.

Don't expect yourself to be able to do all the jobs, all the time. We've got to be able to rely on others. We've got to be able to have teams or coworkers that we can work together with to achieve things. Our school teaches 30 classes per week. There's absolutely no way that I could teach 30 classes per week. Not with having other aspects of the business to run, being able to physically do it, or my mental sanity. Having a solid team to rely on is one of the keys of success.

You know that old saying, "if you want to go fast, go alone, if you want to go far, go together." Well, there's some serious wisdom to that.

## WORK HARD AND SMART

"Work smarter not harder."

I disagree. Sometimes you've got to really grind and work hard. And sometimes you get more efficient about what you're doing.

You've got to work hard and work smart.

Anything you can do to improve a task or a system takes away from some of the hard work and makes us smarter. But that doesn't mean you can let off the gas and stop working hard. You just direct your energy in a different way. Yes, you should absolutely work smart when you can and make your systems more efficient. If you can make a task easier or find a better way to get it done, by all means, do it.

Hard work pays off. That's all there is to it. I'm not telling you to go out and sacrifice every ounce of personal time that you ever have, but just make sure you work hard enough so that at the end of the day when you really stop and think about it, you know you did a good job. If you're a business owner then you know you've got to work hard to make that business grow. Yes, sometimes you've got to work very smart to make sure you're taking advantage of every opportunity you can. They've got to go hand-in-hand.

Fact is, if you aren't working hard or smart, you've got no one to blame but yourself. You aren't going to get promotions or new business from being lazy.

# BUSINESS THOUGHTS

I'm not a business genius. But I work at it. My ability to work and complete tasks consistently can make up for some of my shortcomings.

Work smart and hard.

Hard work pays off.

Communication with your clients and your coworkers is huge.

Be consistent, it builds trust and reliability.

If you work on a team, make sure you're pulling your weight.

There're always things out there you don't know, educate yourself.

When things are running smoothly and positively with your career, it makes it easier for things to be smooth in other areas of your life too. We may all have different careers or ideas in business, but that's the same as when we work on earning a black belt. We all have to do it in our own way. Stay consistent.

Get a coach. There are people out there that will help you up your game. They are motivators, educators, and people that have done it before you. Take advantage of their knowledge.

Know your value! If your value isn't being met then figure out why? Do you have an overinflated view of yourself or are you legit not being valued? When you have an honest answer, make your moves from there. Maybe you aren't in the right place or maybe you need to speak up more.

Put in the work. Put the work into yourself, into your career, into your coworkers, and into your clients.

# CHAPTER ELEVEN
## PURPLE BELT

The lessons you learn can hit you in the oddest of places.

I had friends visiting from out of town for a work event. We were driving home after several hours of training and I got a phone call from an old student of mine.

I still make an effort to speak to many of my senior students who have moved on. Even if it's checking in every few weeks via text, I've always felt it's important that they still feel supported. However, it was a random time for him to call me, in the late afternoon on a Friday, so I asked my friends if they minded if I picked up the call. The short version of the conversation went something like this.

"Mr. Nichols, if you've got a few minutes, I need your advice on something. I'm kind of at a crossroads where I'm trying to make a decision to play it safe and keep going to school in the medical field or go back to pursuing my dream and work on opening my own gym."

He went on to talk for a few minutes about what he was faced with. I interjected a few comments or questions here or there. He talked about the difficult time he was having and making this major life decision. The medical profession was very important to his family and even his culture, but his heart and his passion had been with personal training and having his own gym for quite some time. At this point I had known this young man for about 17 years and had watched him go from a tiny little kid to a hulking mass of muscle. He was hard-working, driven, and passionate about his field.

"Well. I hear everything that you're saying to me bud, I know you're calling for my advice, but quite frankly I don't think I'm going to say anything different then you've just said to me in the last few minutes. I think you've already made the decision; I understand you might be afraid to make that final decision and are almost looking for permission, but I can't give you that permission. This is your life and you will know what the right decision is."

I could hear the emotion in his voice on the other end of the phone. "Thank you, Mr. Nichols. I really appreciate your time. You've always been there for me. I love you."

When I hung up the phone there was a little bit of silence and I said to my friends "Sorry guys, I just somehow knew he was going to need to talk to me." Of course they didn't mind me taking the call or the personal nature of it.

Several months later I was shocked to learn one of my friends from that day had left his job. A job where I had known him for quite some time. It was pretty upsetting as this part of his profession was how we formed a friendship. One afternoon we were discussing the situation and why he left. There were of course many, many reasons, but there is one thing that he said that stuck with me.

"Do you remember that phone call you got that one afternoon we were in the car?" He asked me. "Yeah, why?' I replied.

"When that young man called you to talk and get your advice, there was no hesitation. I could tell there was an incredible bond between the two of you, and he came to you as if you were his own parent. You really are a leader and he knew that. I want to have those types of relationships. I'm never going to have that where I'm at. So, I decided it was time to leave."

It honestly shook me a bit. There was a part of me that was hurt if I was even a small portion responsible for why my dear friend left his job. However, in hindsight, after thinking about his words and further discussion, I understand in that moment it was my example of leadership and the bonds that I grew and demonstrated that affects other people, even when I did not intend to.

Being a leader means that you lead and affect people even when you don't realize it. It was a reminder that others see me as a leader too. Even the people I look up to.

Oh, and the guy with the decision to make. He opened the gym and training center and he's doing great.

# CHAPTER TWELVE

# EARN A BLACK BELT IN LEADERSHIP

What does it mean to be a leader? That's something I'm not sure of sometimes myself. I know in all the years that I've been teaching martial arts the definition of this has changed for me many times. I think even if you don't think of yourself as a "Leader," it doesn't mean that other people don't look to you as one. It's not always about your position in an organization, a company, or even a group of friends. How you carry yourself is what makes you a leader to others.

There're also different types of leaders. A sergeant isn't any less of a leader even though he's not a general. They are just a different type, with different responsibilities and different roles, but not any less important. Still carrying a certain amount of responsibility with it. There is a great responsibility that comes with being a leader. Whether you want the responsibility or not, it just comes with the territory.

# RESPONSIBILITY

I am a person that believes it is your responsibility to put your absolute best into the things you do. We are talking about your job, your relationships, your hobbies. Why would you commit to doing something and do anything less than your best? It wastes your time. Something we've got a limited amount of. Does everyone around us act that way? No, of course not.

But think about it for a second.

If you're consistently putting your best effort and focus into these things that you do, then you are going to benefit from it. Those benefits could be financial, emotional, physical, and very personal. If you are feeling fulfilled because you're getting things done and accomplishing things, then you are reaping the benefits. Also, the effort you're putting into this makes you a leader to others. Whether you mean to or not.

Sure, there are days that I'm not feeling 100%. There are days when I might be in a bad mood, tired, not feeling well and don't want to put my best foot forward. The responsibility of leadership often forces me to have to step up. That stepping up leads to a more fruitful life. No, it's not always easy, and it's not always pleasant, but it definitely makes the positive times even better and the benefits that I reap from my hard work make it all worthwhile. So that responsibility of leadership benefits me, but it also benefits the people around me.

If I take my responsibility to do my best seriously, I have the potential to inspire others. If I take it seriously, I benefit my teammates, co-workers and clients. As a business owner I have a responsibility to my clients and staff.

You could take it a step further and even get into your responsibility to your fellow man. Strangers. People thousands of miles away in other countries. Volunteer work is fulfilling, helpful to others, and an example that can be set to inspire others to help out. If you saw a person in need, would you help them? If you saw a person in danger? Or would you stand by and watch? A leader knows what they would do.

## LEAD BY EXAMPLE

Lead by example. It's a cliché, I know. But that doesn't mean that it's not true. Regardless of your position in a company, your hard work and effort contributes to that company. Your hard work is your example for others. You may not even realize that you're the one that's inspiring someone else to work harder. You might not even realize that the example that you're setting is inspiring someone else to want to achieve more.

The way you carry yourself and the things that you do can be an example of leadership for others. I am a firm believer in "if you show up on time, you're already late." When we have events at my school, I would say 99.9% of the time I am the first one there. How can I ask other people to show up on time and be prepared if I'm not setting an example by doing it? You can call that another cliché example, but again, does it mean it's not true? You can even say it's common sense, but how many people do you know are consistently late for things that are important? If you're a person that runs a team or is a member of a team or an organization it might seem like an insignificant thing, but it's something that goes noticed when it doesn't happen. Think. Do you hear comments about the person that's always on time? Or do you hear complaints about the person that's always late?

## SPEAK UP

I was torn about where to put this in the book because it's going to be helpful for many sections. You've got a voice. Use it.

One of the biggest pieces of advice I can give you is to learn to use your voice. Being able to speak up for yourself, but also in being comfortable talking to people. Speaking to others one on one. In small groups, and even large groups. If you can develop the skills and confidence to be able to speak with purpose, you will go far.

Think of the person that stands in front of a whole group and gives a speech. Think how you feel about the speaker that is low key and drones on. Is this a person that inspires you? Do they make you want to hear and learn what they are saying? Compare them to the dynamic speaker that moves around and projects their voice. That is ok with humor and can drive their point home.

Which would you follow?

Now, I know this is much easier said than done. I know it is a huge skill to develop and takes time. I can also promise you that building confidence in your speaking and talking to others will be something that pays off in life.

You don't have to prepare to go speak to thousands of people, but at least be confident in speaking to a boardroom or a classroom. Knowing how to be enthusiastic without being silly, being loud without yelling, or being clear without being boring will develop those leadership skills.

It sounds silly but you can start by learning to tell a story. Or even read aloud and focus on making it sound like you are talking and not reading. Projecting your voice without yelling. Tell the story! Stories are exciting, somber, captivating. So put the emotion into the moments that need it. Once you can get through reading a book out loud this way, talking to a group is much easier.

If you are working on talking to a small group or an individual, ask people questions. Engaging in asking others questions is a great way to start a conversation or to keep one going. When it's your turn to speak make sure your answers are more than one word. Engage in the conversation. Just like learning to tell a story you have to put some emotion into the conversation. You want a captive audience, not a captured one. So, make sure you are including them in the conversation and not just monopolizing it.

The person that can confidently speak is the person others will look at too. So, if you want to develop leadership skills, learn to use that voice.

## YOU ACTUALLY SHOULD WORRY ABOUT WHAT OTHER PEOPLE THINK OF YOU

I know, I know, you shouldn't worry about what other people think of you. But I think that's all a matter of perspective. No, you should not worry about what haters think about you. However, I do think you should worry about what certain people think of you.

You should be concerned about what their perception of you is. Perception might not always be true, but it's basically the thought that somebody else has in their mind. So, the question is, based on what you're putting out in the world and the way you interact with other people, what is their perception of you? Do people perceive you to be a hard worker? Do they perceive you to be obnoxious? Do they perceive you to be outgoing?

Again, their perception may not necessarily be true, from your point of view. But it could be completely true from their point of view. Anyone in a leadership role has to care about this to an extent. Don't get your feelings hurt by the whole thing, but people's perception of you, based on your actions, your efforts, the way you speak, and the things you say, is very important to your effectiveness as a leader.

You may not even realize some of your behaviors are influencing other people's perceptions of you. Your point of view on how you act and why you act a certain way may be perceived as something totally different.

For example, I have had a few experiences where I have been told I am dismissive. That someone wanted to speak to me and they felt I was dismissive of them. My point of view. I'm fast. I walk fast, I talk fast, I think fast. When I'm hustling back and forth from my office to the workout floor I am moving. If I have to speak to someone it's usually pretty quick and I move on. In my mind I'm trying to help that person and move on to the floor to teach, in their mind, I'm being dismissive. It took me a few times of hearing this from people until I thought about their perception of the situation. Once I saw it from their point of view, I tried to adjust.

Try this for an exercise. Take a serious moment to sit down and think about yourself. Write down 5 to 10 words that you would use to describe yourself. Not how you want to be, but how you honestly are. Then go take five people that know you really well and ask them for three words they would use to describe you. Take it a step further, go ask some people that you are just acquaintances with. Tell them it's an exercise that you're doing and ask for their help. Get three words from them based on what they know about you. Take this information and see how it starts to add up. You could do it with your peers, your subordinates, people based on the different relationships you have. Once you see how other people's perception of you lines up with your own self-image, you may end up being surprised and want to make some adjustments.

The image that you put out there for other people, the things you say and do, your actions, all affect your image. Your image also affects the way you are perceived as a leader. Those actions and images that you put out in the world are also going to attract a specific type of follower. Let's call it the way it is, in our world in the last few years we've had some very polarizing leaders. Regardless of if you like them or not, obviously a great deal of people did. Those leaders' opinions, actions, and attitude drew their followers to them based on the perception of what they were putting out in the world.

## SO WHY BE A LEADER?

You may not set out to be a leader, but you may end up being one. That may be on a small scale or a large one. In my journey, I've formed the opinion that developing leadership skills can be one of the most beneficial things that we can do. You can look at that from the point of view of the good of others or just good for ourselves. Yes, there are different types of leaders. Like we said earlier there are global leaders that shape our countries. Coaches and teachers that have influenced us through our years. All the way down to someone that we work with, who might not be the most vocal person in the room, but their reliability and hard work is an inspiration.

Don't get me wrong, there are plenty of days where I honestly don't want to be the person in charge. Where I don't want to have others look to me for decisions. I'm human. I'm allowed to be tired or frustrated. When you develop leadership skills you sometimes can't help when you are needed or need to step up. There's a responsibility that comes with it. However, I know that the benefits to my life and the life of others far outweigh my mood at the time. I get much more out of knowing that I have a positive impact on others, adding value to their lives and my own.

Just like some of the other chapters in this book, the development of leadership skills is going to improve every area in your life. Leaders take time to grow as well. They need opportunities to evolve. A leader works hard. A leader is mindful of those around them. They are wise when they speak, they admit their mistakes. They can motivate others, and influence our lives.

I've heard it said before, "a good leader does not create followers, they create more leaders."

# CHAPTER THIRTEEN
# BROWN BELT

So, at the time I had been running my school for about 12 years. I owned my own home. Other than a mortgage, I had no debt at all. Things were great with my marriage and my kid was happy and healthy. Absolutely nothing to complain about.

Yet here I was, completely miserable. Stressed out. Depressed. Having anxiety attacks every few days. No real reason why.

The everyday hustle and bustle of owning a business, running it, teaching classes, and all the normal pressures of life had me completely burnt out.

I even reached a point where I really just wanted to sell my school. Absolutely no idea what I would've done beyond that, but I just didn't want to deal with any of it anymore. I'm not saying I was suicidal or anything like that, but the anxiety was just absolutely destroying me and my motivation.

After a few months of just repeating these patterns and issues I fortunately reached a point where I knew I just needed some help.

When I was younger, I had done therapy for several years. I can very openly admit that I have a lot of anger issues from growing up. Still to this day, I have problems with anxiety and do not always do well dealing with stress.

So, at the time, when I finally realized I needed to make some big changes to keep my career on path, I went out and got the help I needed. That came in the form of anxiety medication and people to talk to.

The way I've always described being on the medication was that if my feelings and anxiety were a raging river, the medication allowed me to put a dam up in the middle of the river. I could still see all the water rushing up to it, but the dam allowed me to take a step back and be able to deal with it all.

I started making some life changes to my health and my habits as well as starting to set up things to do when my anxiety was triggered. Eventually I was able to get off the medication and trust in the hard work that I put in.

That doesn't mean that I still don't deal with those things from time to time.

Fast forward from that moment in time to the very first time my family and I decided to fly overseas. After a trip to America for Sami combat systems and its founder, Peter Weackuf and his wife and partner Irmi, my family had decided we would fly back over with them so I could train at headquarters in Vienna and then we would visit several other countries in Europe.

At this point I had only ever traveled to Florida on trips to Disney World. Traveling to the other side of the world, to a country that I did not speak the language or know very much about the culture, wanting to train and impress my instructor and friends. I must've almost completely broken down from the anxiety a dozen times before we even flew over. I wasn't afraid to fly or anything like that. It was all the unknowns and uncertainty about traveling to a foreign country and training in a different environment.

I heavily needed to rely on my organizational skills, communicating my feelings openly with trusted friends, and the systems I put in place to deal with my anxiety. Everything ended up working out just fine. Since then, I've been fortunate enough to travel to many different countries and parts of the world. And every single time I start prepping for one of these trips, there's always a certain amount of stress and anxiety that comes with it for me. I've been able to learn to work through it, but it still always rears its head.

If I never learned to overcome the stresses and challenges of daily life, I know there's a great many things that I would've missed out on. Even though many of these things are simple, normal life experiences, they are still the stresses I have to deal with. We all wrestle with our own demons.

# CHAPTER FOURTEEN

# EARN A BLACK BELT IN MENTAL HEALTH

We've got to get our heads right.

You can call it "mental health." You can call it "self-love." "You can keep it really simple and just call it "taking care of yourself." Taking control of your mental and physical attitude is incredibly important. If my previous stories are any indication, this is something I'm still earning a black belt in. Truth is, you never stop earning a black belt, and you're always working toward it. As you deal with the ups and downs of life, you're still working on your mental health.

Depression, anxiety, stress, dealing with trauma, there's so many different ways that we need to be mindful of how we feel and how to deal with it. There's more focus nowadays on mental health than there ever has been in our history. There was easily a time when "suck it up" was really about the most recognition you got for something when you were stressed out or having emotional difficulties dealing with it. At least today there is a lot more focus on the subject and opportunities to get help.

# MENTAL HEALTH IS NOT A WEAKNESS

Let's get this straight first, whatever stigma you can think of about mental health, get that right out of here. There's no shame in needing help. There's no shame in needing therapy, there's no shame in needing medication, there's no shame in leaning on others. The only issue is if you're doing those things but not doing any of the work on your problems. The whole stigma around mental health is garbage. These things are real and we all deal with them to different degrees. There's absolutely nothing wrong with that.

Some of the issues that we deal with can be minor, and some can be absolutely paralyzing. Things like anxiety can range from just getting a little bit nervous in certain situations all the way to causing you to completely shut down when something triggers you. Maybe there's a reason for your anxieties, and maybe there's not. It could just be something that you deal with. Whatever the situation is, there's nothing wrong with that happening, there's just something wrong if you don't do anything about it. Don't allow yourself to live like that. You are worth more than that.

Not to mention if you're not taking care of yourself mentally, if you're not giving yourself breaks from the hard work and effort, if you're not finding ways to work through your problems, then all the other areas we previously read about are going to be limited. How are you going to excel at your job if you're still dealing with the anxiety you get when it comes to talking to other people? How are you going to teach your kid to grow up confident and believing in themselves if you don't believe in yourself? How can you move forward in a healthy relationship if you don't deal with the trauma that you experienced in an earlier one? Whatever your situation may be, you get my point.

## WHAT ARE YOU HOLDING ONTO?

Often much of the pain and anxieties we have are from past traumas we are still holding onto. Regrets and our hold onto past events are preventing us from moving forward. Those events from our past are still haunting us and we haven't moved on.

Are the regrets you have of your past really worth wrecking your future? In most cases what is it? A bad relationship? One ending we didn't want to end? Behavior we regret? Someone wronging us?

These things don't serve us. Just because we didn't get the closure we wanted isn't a reason to let something in the past dictate our future. Yes, we should absolutely learn from these experiences. In some ways learning a lesson is a form of closure.

Okay so if you are holding onto regret or past demons you've got to do one of those deep dives of honesty and rip it out. You've got to set aside some time and wrestle with what you're holding onto. The how's, who's, and why's that will get you to sit and deal with it. I know we all know this, but you can't change the past. You can only deal with it now.

Okay yes, depending on your personal situation you can go back and talk to people and try to set things right or get closure, but still, you can't change what has happened in the past, just deal with it now.

But getting clear on what you're holding onto and dealing with is how you learn and move forward.

Be ready though! When you are dealing with it you are not going to like all the answers. If you did then you wouldn't still be holding onto it and letting it cause you pain. So, accept it's not going to be easy, be ready to sort through some difficult feelings. But you are sorting through it for closure, to learn, to move on.

And that's what you have to eventually do. Accept your findings and move on. Unburdened by your regrets. Sorting through the pains of our past is the only way we can move unburdened into our future. To do so healthily we have to learn from our past. Learn from our regrets. Leave them behind us.

Self-evaluations, discussing it with others, or even getting help is a start.

## HELP IS OUT THERE

So, are the things you are working through able to be dealt with on your own, or is it something you need to seek professional help for? Time to do another one of those self-evaluation. Are you dealing with things that you can set up action steps to work through, or are you dealing with something that would be best left to the help of a professional? This might be something you can decide on your own or it might be something that you need help with. Remember a couple of chapters ago when we talked about vulnerability? Open up to someone you're close to about your situation. They might have some great ideas on how to work through it, or they might agree and think that you need a pro.

Maybe you just need a little support. Just having a circle of friends or an organization that you can belong to and get some support can help.

I belong to a men's group. It's an online organization called, "Berserker Beards Club Inc." It's an online group of bearded men from all over the world who do charity work as well as a support group. Truthfully, there's a large amount of time where it's just a bunch of guys talking online, busting each other's chops and having a good couple of laughs. But as soon as someone brings up something serious, every single person in that group's attitude changes and all of a sudden, it's a group of men listening to each other, offering advice, and most importantly, support. No judgment, just support. Since I joined, I have had several situations that I opened up to the club about. My father went through a very drastic and shocking medical situation that went on for almost 6 months. During that time, I was hearing from different club members on a weekly basis, checking in and giving me support. Although none of these men were physically there, it was great to know that I had people I could open up to and that were there for me anytime I needed someone to talk to. I guarantee if I did need someone, several members would have jumped on a plane. Their brotherhood helped me through that time.

Finding a support group to have that outlet and to give you others to lean on can be a massive help and a great comfort when you need it. Just like building those relationships in your life, a support group is a special kind of relationship. One where you and the other members in it have things that tie you together that quite possibly other people in your life just possibly couldn't understand. Remember that it's OK to lean on these people, that's why you're all in the support group together.

A support group may not be right for you. Maybe you're the type of person that does better opening up to someone one on one. There are plenty of therapists, psychologists, and mental health specialists out there to help you. In the later part of high school and my first couple of years of college I was in therapy weekly. There's absolutely nothing wrong with having an outside source that you can use as your sounding board on the things that you're working through. More often than not these people are asking questions to get you to think about them. They're asking you things so that you can evaluate yourself and come to your own conclusions. Also keep in mind that getting into therapy can take some time. The first therapist you go to might not be the right one for you. Like any other relationship it takes time to develop understanding and trust with this person. Don't be afraid to do some research until you find someone that just clicks for you.

There's also nothing wrong just talking to a doctor and trying to figure out if medication is right for you. As I explained previously there was a period of time in my life where I was on medication to help with my anxiety. It's happened to me twice in my life where I was just having a hard time getting a grip on everything and getting on proper medication helped me be able to work through it. Now in my specific case, I used the medication so I could set up other routines and ideas to be able to handle my stress and anxiety so I could get off of the medication. I used it for a certain amount of time to educate myself, work through my difficulties, and put myself in a better position so I would no longer need medication. Everyone is different. There are some people that just might need to help keep on meds long term to keep themselves straight. Under the supervision of a doctor that's not necessarily a bad thing. Getting help isn't a weakness. It takes strength to admit we need help, and even more to go get it.

Remember back in the business chapter where I talked about my small group of friends that touches base weekly? We talk about what we are working on and how we are educating ourselves. We also use this time as a check in for anything else going on in our lives. My buddy Jake and I speak weekly. It's a motivating phone call. We discuss work, our families, and what we are up to. Every time we speak, I get off the phone feeling good. Even if I'm dealing with difficulties in my life, having a motivating person to speak to makes me feel supported. Even if it's just a person that's a sounding board for my ideas and what I'm up to. Find that friend that you can speak to that makes you feel good about yourself.

## PERSPECTIVE

How many things have you ever experienced in your life, or how many times have you ever had a problem that the next day, sometimes even just an hour later, ends up really not being that big of a deal? We get hit with a problem that we completely freak out about and instantly get stressed out, only to be able to solve it rather easily within a short amount of time. I would venture to say that the mass majority of the things in our lives that we end up having to "deal with" end up really not being that big of a deal. We end up solving our problems, working through them, and finding solutions with it all working out much better than we originally thought it was going to. At the time it was a huge deal. It was a massive pain that we had to deal with and were even super negative about. But it got sorted out and we moved on.

Yes, some things are absolutely a big deal that end up leaving us with emotional scars or life-changing situations. With a little time and some perspective how many things do we end up dealing with that end up not being a big deal at all? However, in the moment when it hits us and we're dealing with it, how many of us jump to instant stress and frustration when thinking about what we are now having to deal with? We get blinders on about the situation very quickly.

Just like in the chapter on organization when we talked about going through your day according to plan and then getting hit with something out of left field. For some people, getting hit with something random can completely ruin their mood, or their day. In the long haul it's just a matter of being able to look at it the right way, solve it, and move on.

I am a person that gets stressed very easily. In all honesty I can end up getting frustrated for the absolute stupidest of things. I get stress and anxiety about dealing with situations that might be slightly out of my control or that I ended up not planning for. It is 100% probably my biggest flaw. I have unnecessary anxiety and stress issues. So, when these things come up, I try my best to battle my frustration, take a deep breath, I try to bite my tongue from saying anything out of snap judgment, and really have a little perspective when looking at the situation. I know when my blood starts pumping and I get frustrated that I'm not usually going to say or do the right thing. So, my first reaction is most often not the right reaction. I've completely learned this about myself, and although I might not catch it all the time, I try to be mindful of it and really stop and look at the situation. Is what I'm getting all bent out of shape over really that big of a deal? Is it something that I can just fix and move on with and forget about? If I'm lucky, a good couple of deep breaths, some good evaluation of the situation, and kicking myself for getting upset over something stupid, allows me to fix it and move right on. Not always. Like I said, this is an area I am still working on.

# TREAT YOURSELF

OK, so you are hard-working. You are on top of your day. You are focused on the task at hand. What do you do to let go? What do you do to treat yourself? You still gotta have relief from time to time. Think of it like a cheat day on a diet. Are you doing things to change your routine and reward yourself from the mental stress that you choose to endure on a daily basis? You can call it a hobby or whatever you want, but you've got to have something that gives you a special type of satisfaction in your week. Why do people go on vacations every now and then?

Because they've earned it.

You've earned it.

You've got to be able to do a little something for yourself every now and then. Yes, there are plenty of people whose entire lives are defined by their job. It's what they're known for, it's what they do, it's what they live for. Fine. Even in those cases you've got to give yourself a breather sometimes.

I'm an avid motorcycle rider. If you've ridden before then you understand, and if you don't ride, you might not be able to understand. There's something meditative about being out on that road. You can be riding in a group or solo. There's just something about you being on that machine with the wind blowing past you and your brain fixated on the road. Just having that meditation allows me to come up with some of my best ideas on some days.

Do you go to the gym? Do you study martial arts? Are you a runner? You should 100% have something physical in your life. I'm not going to write an entire chapter on the physical benefits of weekly activity, we all know what they are by now. Exercise also benefits you mentally. Increased oxygen, the stress relief, the way you feel good about yourself after a workout. You may not necessarily think of this as treating yourself, but it's definitely good maintenance that you should be doing. You should even take this moment to stop and ask yourself if you are moving enough. Do you have physical activity? Is it good enough? I'm not saying you should be a gym rat and hitting the gym six days a week, I mean if that's your thing, all good, but I'm saying you've at least got to have something physical in your life. Doing 10 sit ups every other day doesn't exactly count either. Getting that heart rate up and getting some physical movement in is definitely going to get the juices flowing.

Your outlet doesn't have to be physical either. A creative outlet is a great way to unwind and relax. You can paint, write music, poetry, or even just as simple as journaling. Start just writing down your thoughts. You don't have to share it with anyone. There are even journals to help you and teach you to start journaling but asking you daily questions. Yes, physical activity is great for your health and your sanity. Having a creative outlet just works the brain differently than a physical one. Some people just have an easier time with this. You have to find an outlet that works for you.

You know what, maybe every now and then you deserve something nice too. I'm not saying go out and sacrifice all of your family finances on that brand new sports car, you can have that as a goal and work toward it, I'm just saying that it's OK to treat yourself every now and then. Use some common sense by giving yourself that little reward every now and then is a nice reminder that your hard work pays off.

Don't ignore this.

If I was going to sum up this chapter, I think it really comes down to two things. First of all, having that balance in life. Work, family, friends, obligations, and your sanity. Finding that work life balance is a really big deal. When one thing is out of balance very often it tips the scales so that something else gets damaged. Making sure you're taking care of yourself physically, mentally, and emotionally really keeps everything running smoothly. Make sure that you've got things going on that make you happy. If you don't, start finding some. Don't be afraid to start small. Don't be afraid to start something and decide it's not for you and switch to something else. And don't be afraid to treat yourself every now and then.

Second, yes, there's almost always going to be someone else in the world with bigger problems than you have. There's going to be someone else that's had it worse. There's always going to be someone else whose scars run deeper than yours. We can be respectful of that and we can try to look on the bright side of our own issues, but our problems, our stresses, our anxieties, our trauma, are still ours. And it's OK to feel bad about it. But do yourself a major favor and do something about it. Learn to work through these things, don't be afraid to get help, and use every resource you can to your advantage. Don't just let your stressors and frustrations run your life, do something about it.

Realizing this can be a long process. It may not be easy. It will have ups and downs. I've had times where I'm on fire for months and months. Working hard, getting things done. Just killing it daily. Then out of nowhere a random negative situation totally throws me off. And the negativity I experience flows into every area of my life. I get distant from my family and friends, my work suffers, my fitness routines fall off track. It happens. It can happen to any of us.

Do I fight back? Of course, I do. After a little time, I find a way to fight my way out of the funk. If I use the tools I've learned along the way and try to keep a little perspective, I'm usually able to bounce back faster. Each time is different. Each time is unpredictable.

But you know what? That's ok. It's ok If I'm working through something. There's no reason to feel bad about it. As long as I'm putting in the work and doing all I can, I'm good. And so are you.

# CHAPTER FIFTEEN

# RED BELT

I have been fortunate to receive many accolades, awards, and recognitions during my career. Sometimes they mean a great deal to me and sometimes they are just something to take up wall space. But I have been incredibly fortunate to have these two successes as of late.

September 1, 2021 was such an odd, surreal, and exciting day. Building up to the day there were reports of massive rain storms and severe weather. I was feverishly deciding on canceling our event or proceeding. As the rain wasn't supposed to hit until much later, I decided to proceed. During one of the worst rain storms in New Jersey history, over 400 people came by the school throughout the evening to help celebrate our 20-year anniversary.

In the pouring rain there were people sitting under tents at tables behind the school, happily eating the catered food, laughing, smiling, and having a great time. There was a line to the ice cream truck of people trying to stay dry while they got some treats. We were jam packed inside the school and all you could hear was laughter and yelling and people having a good time. The mayor had come by, the local news crew had come by, former students who I had not seen in years came by as well.

In the pouring down rain over the course of several hours, hundreds of people came by to celebrate the community that had been built on the back of 20 years of hard work. It's funny, 20 years and it's never felt like it. I think that's why it's always been very surreal to me. It's always hard to imagine how many people I've interacted with and taught over 20 years.

I was proud to have my daughter there that night. It meant a great deal to me to be able to see her on the floor teaching alongside all my other staff members, and standing beside me while I was interviewed for television. I was given a wonderful plaque to hang on the wall from the mayor. I'm proud to see it hanging alongside several of the other awards and our accolades that our school has received over the years. All the awards are great and all, but it's the support of family, friends and students that mean the most.

Fast forward a few months to January 16, 2022. We were holding a black belt test. Every black belt test is special. Every time you have one there are students and people there that have worked for years and years building up to that moment. Although I really do try to get people to understand that earning your black belt is by far not the end of things, it's certainly a huge achievement, and the culmination of years of work and dedication. The black belt mindset should be one that understands that there is still much more to learn.

This exam was a very special one for me. It wasn't the largest exam that we had ever held, it did not have the highest ranks that I ever tested. But it was special because my own daughter was testing. She was testing alongside several students and staff members that also hold a special place in my heart. The event was attended by friends of hers who traveled some distance to come watch, and ended up sitting for over seven hours watching the exam. It was attended by friends of mine and former students that had literally come in from all across the country. It really may have been the greatest gathering of my students that we have ever had. Some members of the panel have been my students for over 20 years. Men and women who started as children and were now doctors, physical therapists, marketing directors, and businessmen themselves.

Admittedly, although the exam was for everyone that was there, of course a good portion of my focus was on the teenage girl that I had once held at the first moments of her life. I must've cried two dozen times throughout the day. Watching her work hard, push herself physically, fight through emotions when she was exhausted, and exceed my expectations, I easily failed to hold back my emotions. It may be a rare thing when you get to have the child that you raised go through an experience that is a part of your own life's path.

At the end of the day when it was time to place the black belt around her waist, few people in the room knew the announcement I would make. As hard as it would be to believe, she was testing for her black belt 20 years to the day after I tested for mine. After fighting through the tears and being able to call her name to come up and receive her rank, I removed the belt that I had worn for 20 years and placed it around her waist.

As much as I know that my job as a parent is far from over. There was just something in that moment that made me feel like my life's path of being a martial arts instructor and a motivator, merged together with my greatest job of all, being a parent. In that moment and as I look back on that day, I cannot think of a greater feeling of success that I've ever held in my life. Although I still have much to work toward and many things to achieve, I know in that moment I was successful in making an impact.

I don't know about you but I've had a couple of times in my life where I've either seen it on TV, read it in a book, or through a deep conversation late one night with a friend, thought about, "if I were to die right now, would I be satisfied with my life?"

I actually thought about that many times. I've even really tried to live in the mindset of if I left this earth right now, have I done good things? I am by no means a perfect man; I really do think of myself as a pretty average guy. Nothing special at all really.

But I do know if I were to leave this earth today, I've been fortunate enough to impact many people and bring a lot of positivity into other peoples' world. I've been able to watch many students grow up and start to achieve their dreams. I've been able to travel and have amazing experiences.

I'm not saying that there still aren't things I want to accomplish or things that I would regret missing out on. I'm just saying that I know I've done good things. If I keep

my mindset of achieving, impacting, and experiencing,
then I know I will keep on a path of living a satisfying life.

# CHAPTER SIXTEEN

# EARN A BLACK BELT IN SUCCESS

This one is going to be different for every single person that reads it. Because in order to earn a black belt in success you first have to be able to define what success means to you. You can think of a successful movie star that makes millions and millions of dollars and whose name is known throughout the entire world. You can think of billionaire tech giants and doctors. You can also think of a person who owns their own home, works a regular 9-to-5, and is happily married with kids. These people are all wildly successful depending on how you define success. You can define it by the amount of money in your bank or you can define it by the amount of freedom you feel like you have in your life. This is all a very personal concept. So, you have to define it and make sure it's got some real success in it. Do you really want all your successes to be mediocre? Is sub-par ok with you? I think if average was ok that you wouldn't be reading a book on motivation and personal growth. People don't try to be mediocre; they settle for it and don't fight their way out.

So admittedly, as I write this chapter, it will be skewed toward my personal views on success. I am not a rich man. I still at times get stressed out about my mortgage and our bills and savings. For the most part we live comfortably, but I am by no means rich. Money may not be able to buy happiness, they say, but let's be honest, it does make some things easier. For me, beyond being able to pay for the things in my life and not having to worry too much about them, financially I don't feel like I need much more. Yes, I want to live comfortably, but I'm not a person that feels like I have to live in abundance. I don't define success financially as having millions and millions of dollars in the bank. It's OK if you do, but for me success comes from other areas. Absolutely you can have both if that is your definition of success.

I've always felt like success is in the quality of the things you do, the people you surround yourself with, and the impact you make on others. I want rich experiences in life. I want to make a difference in other people's lives. I want to leave my mark on the world.

## WHAT ARE YOU WORKING FOR?

We spend the mass majority of our life working, don't we? It could be for ourselves or someone else, but we still spend an awful lot of time working and trying to make money. We can go back to talking about working harder or smarter, but the mass majority of us are still working. So, my question is, what are you working for? Are you working because your idea of success is a large amount of money? Are you working because you want a big home, fancy cars, lots of cool stuff in the house? Are you working because you want to be able to retire early and relax and do nothing? If these are some of the ways that you define success, then you need to make sure you have a game plan to get there.

Saving for retirement, investing, owning property, and all those other big crazy financial concepts are some of those subjects that when my friends are talking about them, I'm just kinda standing there staring and nodding my head up and down. Admittedly a lot of that is way over my head. Yes, over some time I've educated myself about it enough, but I'm also smart enough to know this is one of those areas where getting help is a big deal.

Let me at least tell you two things I know. First off, start saving early. start saving early on in your life. If you are older and you haven't, start now. I wish I had started saving for my financial future about 10 years earlier than I did. So, what did I do with all that money? I spent it on garbage. That's the second thing. What are you really spending your money on? Yes, you should absolutely treat yourself sometimes.

Sometimes!

But don't spend the majority of your money on garbage all the time. Enjoy things in life but look at what you are spending your money on. Make some adult decisions.

If part of your definition of success is making sure your financial future is going in the right direction, then you've got to make sure to find that help to get there. Find a coach, find a financial planner, talk to a friend who's got more knowledge about this than you do, but get it done.

Financial focus might not be your focus. A job to you just might be a means to an end. A way to pay your bills and have things in your life but not necessarily the thing that you're working for. Does the impact that you make on other people bring you more joy than anything else in your life? I know people who completely live for volunteer work. They completely live for finding causes to help and focusing on the benefits to mankind. This is what they want for their life. These people don't find success by their financial future, but they work for the impact that they make on others. This is how they define success.

When you think about what you're working for it might not even be such a black-and-white area. It might be a bit more general. Yes, you could be working for your family. Working on setting up their future. That can absolutely be financial, it can be your home and your children's education, and their safety. This could be the thing that you feel defines your success. What do you need to make sure that you're financially sound if you're going to be taking care of your family's future? You have to be making an impact on your children to be helping to guide them properly. You have to be putting effort into your relationships in order to keep the family unit whole.

All this comes down to how you define success. What values, ideas, and goals you have for your life. Once these are defined you can move in a direction.

## WHAT ARE YOU LOOKING AT?

Your definition of success can also be explained not by what you're working for, but what you're looking at. I mean are you looking at short-term or long-term. Are you looking at the whole of your life, or are you looking at this concept moment to moment? Do you feel good? Are you happy? Relatively speaking with success can also be defined by your definition of your general happiness. If your job is consistent and positive, if the relationships around you are good, if your mental health is relatively under control, all these things can lead to your general happiness. So maybe instead of just looking at the whole picture, we really just need to look at our day to day.

No, every day is not going to be perfect, and bad things happen in life. We can get aggravated about things; we can't have everything be positive. I'm talking about our overall happiness. Are things mostly working out for you and are you generally having a good time day to day, are your interactions with other people mostly positive? Are you treating yourself and doing things that you generally enjoy? I think that if we can check the boxes for the most part on a daily basis then we're doing a pretty good job. I'm not saying that there aren't going to be struggles, and I'm not saying that you shouldn't hustle, what I'm saying is that if we're making the effort and getting things done in our life, having a good impact, and having a little fun, I think we're pretty successful. Sometimes you've got to have a little perspective.

If we can check enough of these days off of being positive and working hard and having good relationships then yes, I think the long-term picture ends up being a successful one as well. As always, self-evaluate and think about this.

## CREATE YOUR SUCCESS

Be clear about your definition of success. Short-term long-term, whatever. If you're really clear about what that definition is, you have something to work toward. I am someone that does a lot better in my day-to-day life if I have a goal. If I have things going on that I'm working toward. Something obtainable, even written down on the calendar as an event. I know if something is on the horizon then I just generally work better in everything that I do.

Take writing this book for example. I've got a deadline; everything has to be done so that puts me in a position to feel like that I need to accomplish things in a certain amount of time so they still have room to go back into the book and make edits and changes and improvements. On top of that when people found out that I was writing a book I then felt responsible for putting even more effort into making sure that I believed in what I was writing. Because other people will be reading this and quite frankly making judgments about my character based on what I write. Also, as I'm writing the book and still living my normal life, I'm constantly having the book reflected in my actions. If I go home and have a stupid fight with my kid I'm forced to think about that chapter on parenting and ask myself how I could've dealt with it differently. Also, I still have a business to run, so I've got to get my normal work done and find time to work on the book. However, I can't do my regular work half-heartedly because then I feel like a hypocrite for writing so much about the effort we put into things.

Having the goal of working on this book has 100% made me step up my game in all areas of my life. Sometime in the next few months when it's done, and even when it's released, I will have a feeling of success. I will feel positive about that success as people buy the book, read it, hopefully like it, and so on. Even further down the road as I get to add "author" to my résumé there's a sense of pride and success in that.

So, by setting the goal to do this, I'm impacting my life, even just by stepping up and taking a risk and just going for it. A great feeling of success comes when we step out of our comfort zone. When we do things, we wouldn't normally do.

# TAKE A LEAP

Again, another cliché! I could take the next few paragraphs to type out all of the clichés about taking a risk, stepping out of your comfort zone, taking a leap of faith. But we should constantly have things in our lives that are forcing us to do something we wouldn't normally do. To work toward a new achievement, to earn a new goal, yes, I hate to say it, to level up. Succeeding is easy! Having the guts to go for something and possibly fail is hard. You can set goals short to make sure they are easier to obtain, or you can have the guts to go for something big!

If we define success by achievements, then by constantly doing all these things will do just that, we achieve success. Writing this book may only take a few months of my life, but once it's done, I have achieved that success. I can move on to something else and set a new goal. I can step out of my comfort zone and do something else with it. But if I'm adding up these achievements, I'm going to have a feeling of success. Once again, that positive feeling of success is going to affect everything in my life and set an example of leadership for others.

Not every goal has to be huge. Several small achievements add up. And as we achieve smaller things, we start to build our confidence about achieving larger things. This is exactly how the belt system in many martial arts schools works. Even if you're not a martial artist I would almost guarantee you've heard that "martial arts helps build confidence." I would even say it builds confidence in a way that very few other activities do. And one of the many ways it accomplishes this is through a school's belt system. Yes, every school is different so I can only speak from my own experience, so here goes.

We have a belt system. White bell, yellow bell, orange bell, so on and so forth. But within those belts you'll see "stripes" that you have to earn on your belt. Pieces of colored tape that recognize that you know a certain amount of the material. So, think of it as the long-term goal of earning a black belt. The medium-term goal of earning your next colored belt rank, and then the short-term goal of earning all those stripes on your belt. See where the confidence comes into play? Because you're constantly setting a goal and working toward achieving something bigger. Can we apply the same principles to our life outside of the martial arts school?

Set goals in this way. Short term, long term, anything. Let's set things up so you're learning and achieving new things. Take that leap on picking up something you always thought about trying. Confidence is often built through achievement. So, setting goals, different types of goals help us to achieve.

"Well what if I fall short?"

Yeah, you might. Remember what I said, "You have to have the guts to possibly fail." You can always readjust the goal and work toward it differently. Or break it down into smaller steps. But just like me writing this book, the effort of going through it and the clear definition of having standards as I work on it is still helping me to achieve better things in my life. This adds to my personal success and my feeling about myself.

## GETTING IN THE WAY OF SUCCESS

Most of the time, not all of the time, but very often, the number one thing that gets in the way of our success is us. We get in our own way. We get stuck in our head and think of 1 million reasons why we can't do something.

I don't have time, I don't have the money, I'm not good enough, I don't know how to get started.

First off, go ahead and think of one of those goals you want to achieve that's lurking around in the back of your mind and ask yourself why you haven't done it yet. Ask yourself what the excuses that kept you from achieving it. In most cases it's just that, an excuse.

Excuses are the lies we tell ourselves to justify our own weakness.

How does one person achieve big things and then another person achieves nothing? We all have the same 168 hours during the week, part of it is just how we use it.

Yes, I know we all have different skill sets, and different situations in our lives. I'm not saying that we're all failures because we aren't all Jeff Bezos. But there's no reason why we can't have success and achieve many of the things that make us feel positive. If we are falling short on these things it's most likely our own fault.

Lack of Drive, lack of effort, lack of self-discipline.

I'm not trying to sit here and tell you why you suck and why you're falling short on things, because trust me I often do the same thing. It's way easier to have an excuse on why you're not going to step up and do something then it is to put in the work and do it. My point is that if we get better at recognizing these excuses and then we have a greater chance of overcoming them and not letting them become a habit.

It's a habit to stay on the couch instead of going out to exercise. It's a habit to fall into a deep dive on Netflix then to engage in our own personal education. And it's not that there's anything wrong with these things, it's about having the balance of doing the things that you should be doing and then doing the things that you may want to do.

## FALL DOWN SEVEN TIMES; GET UP EIGHT

Can't have black without white. You can't have day without night. You can't have wrong without right. (Is that a song?) You can't have success without failure. Failure is part of success. You cannot separate it. You are not going to succeed in everything you do the first time every time. Falling short of a goal or failing to do it is not complete failure. It's just part of the story on your path to success. Sometimes the failure and the buildup make the success that much greater.

There's also even something to be said about learning more from falling short of a goal than there is from just achieving it the first time. If you achieved everything the first time then your mindset might end up being, "well the way I prepare for everything is perfect."

Where if you fall short of something and have to reevaluate the goal, you're forced to think about it. You're forced to solve problems from a different point of view. You may even end up working that much harder the second time.

Don't see your falling short as a negative. It's part of the path of growth. It's part of your story. Your mindset is everything. If you have a mindset of failure then you're going to consistently fall short and be disappointed. If you work on a mindset of achieving success, when you fall short, you will still look for the positives and be able to reevaluate. Your perception on the matter will determine how it turns out. If you keep looking at everything as a negative then it's going to be negative. If you look for the positive in it, learn from the experience, and push forward, then you are already successful. Your mindset really matters. Yes, this is sometimes easier said than done, but like everything else, it's a habit. And you are in control of your habits. Your good ones, your bad ones. All of them. If you have a bad habit, it's because you're choosing to have a bad habit and support that habit. If you have a good habit, it's because you developed the positive self-control to be able to have that good habit. Having a good habit of positive focus and success is completely within your control.

## MOTIVATION AND DISCIPLINE

Your motivation will be part of what helps get you there. Your "Why." Why did you get started/ What are you looking for? Go back to that section that talked about your definition of success and what you are trying to achieve. But motivation is a big deal. Everyone gets motivated differently. Sometimes my personal motivation can be the rocket fuel to get me through hours and hours of work. And sometimes it wanes and I can barely use it to get me out of bed. When motivation fails, discipline is what keeps you going.  So, both need to be developed.

Get your psych up music playlist together. Write down every motivational quote you read. Any little cliche meme or pic you see that gives you a kick in the butt. Collect it all. All that stuff adds up. Who's your motivating friend? Who are those people you can call that make you feel like you can conquer the world? Use all of that. Use anything that makes you want to get out there and just kill your day.

Use that motivational energy to get things done. Use it to get yourself in the good habits of accomplishing your day. Because there are going to come times when your motivation just isn't there. Days when you're just off your game. Those are the days you are going to be thankful of the self-discipline you developed getting all those things done. You use the motivation to develop the discipline. You use discipline on the days you aren't feeling motivated

## WRAP UP

So, if you think back to the earlier chapters, how did I go from the depressed kid and teen I was when I was younger to the award winning, black belt earning, confident entrepreneur that I am today?

Maybe a lot of luck.

Definitely making some good decisions and having some good people in my life. But I believe it really came down to learning to set goals and work toward them. Learning to achieve small goals to build confidence to go for larger ones. When you work toward things and achieve them you build confidence. A constant "I can" attitude will take you far. That doesn't mean I didn't fall short along the way. Of course, I've stumbled. But I was able to gain confidence through re-evaluating and adjusting goals. I also think I was learning to like myself. You need to like the person you are. And the person you are becoming along your path. Once you like that person then you want to see them succeed and will help them along the path.

In some cases, there isn't really a clear path to success. It's all determined by how we define our success, if we are looking at short-term or long-term goals, and quite frankly how we feel about ourselves. I think if you're doing good things, if you're setting goals and working toward them, if you're trying to be a positive influence on others, then you've already got a good deal of success. It's just a matter of what you set those goals for, how hard you're working to achieve them, and the quality of the relationships you have. In your own way, the more you want, the more you work for, the more you will have.

# CHAPTER SEVENTEEN

# BLACK BELT

Writing this book has been such an amazing experience. Not necessarily an easy one, but definitely a great one. I really don't understand how a person that is writing a multi hundred-page book with a story can actually do it. It's absolutely insane. So, props to them.

Basically, the way I've described it to people is this:

Think about a subject in your life. Think about something that you know pretty well. For example, I'm just gonna say, OK, you're a mechanic, do you know how to change oil? Pretty simple for you. In fact, I bet you know a lot of information about it. You can tell me a lot of things about changing oil, types of oil, filters, how it's changed over the years. You get the idea.

OK, now take everything that you know about that subject and write it down on paper. All of a sudden you realize everything you thought you knew only takes up two or three pages.

So, for me, as I've looked through the subjects in this book and the things that I've wanted to share, that

I've learned on my path, to help others, I've really been forced to take a deep dive into a lot of them. Not only that, but as I sit and write these chapters, it's really forced me to hold a mirror up to myself and make sure that I can live up to the things I'm writing about.

I can't suggest to you, or tell you how to earn a black belt in anything if I'm not putting in the work myself. So, as I've been working on this book I've been constantly evaluating, readjusting, and working on things myself. There are still things I'm earning my black belt in.

But I think it's important to know that making improvements and changes is always a choice. I refuse to just be an observer in my own life. I want to make changes and have experiences that make it all worthwhile.

Now here's a few things I'll let you in on:

Black belt isn't something you just earn, it's something you become.

The years of dedication, focus, and hard work it takes to earn a black belt in martial arts is also about the person that you become. I don't see that being any different than what we've discussed here. While you're working to earn your successes in life, you become successful. While you work on improving the relationships around you, you end up being in good relationships. As you work on your mental health, you become healthy.

I guess in some ways it's that whole, "it's not the destination but the journey,"
Because here's something else:

Black belt is not a destination. You are continually working to earn your black belt. Every single day. Black belt isn't about mastery, it's about the effort of mastery.

Take any chapter in this book, take any idea that you're working toward, and the achievement of it is only based on the effort that you put into it.

It doesn't matter who you are, it doesn't matter where you are in life, if you want to improve anything you read about in this book, you just have to put in the effort. Make the decision, create the mindset, and put in the effort. That's why this is, "an average guy's guide to life." Because, I am just a man, just a human. No different from you. On this earth, just trying to exist. We all have a story. It's called our lives. We are in control of that story. No, it's not always a happy story. There are challenges and obstacles, but we can make the choices of how that story goes. So, we might as well put in the effort to enjoy it and do something good with it.

Not long ago my father ended up having to have both of his legs amputated above the knee. One leg, and then the other one several months later. Completely unrelated reasons. I don't know if I will ever be able to find a way to put into words the emotion and the shock of the situation that we went through for months. I just remember that every day the only thing I could do was be there at his side and help keep him moving forward.

I will never forget that one afternoon we were sitting in the car in a parking lot waiting for my stepmother. He was understandably deeply depressed at that point, deeper than I've ever seen him be before. Even though he had already been paralyzed for 10 years, that step back rarely slowed him down. He was still very active; we spent a lot of time with friends. It was after he became paralyzed that he built his motorcycle. A monstrous handicap tricycle with a suicide shifter and a mount for his wheelchair on the back. He could throw that monster into second gear and pop wheelies on it. But when it came time to have his legs amputated, this blow was completely different to him. Even though he wasn't really using his legs, losing them was unfathomable.

At one point he said to me, "Son, I'm not gonna have any legs. I just don't even know what to do. I don't know how I'm gonna keep living like this."

I replied, "Just gonna keep doing it one day at a time. We will figure this out. I'm telling you dad this will all end up being okay."

I will never forget when he looked me dead in the eyes and said, "How the hell are you always so positive?"

I replied, "Well Dad, I've got to be something, I might as well be positive. Besides, you love me anyway."

"Yeah, I'm not so sure about that anymore."

Through the tears we both burst out laughing. It was a moment of bonding that I will always be thankful for. While he dealt with his pain, me trying to keep things positive in that moment was what we both needed.

My point being, if you've got to be something, you might as well try and be positive. No, it's not always easy, and trust me, I fail at it all the time. But I try.

Almost all of the problems we face in life can be solved. Almost all of the things that make us upset end up getting sorted out. So, we might as well just try to keep things positive and keep moving forward. Yes, I say almost because we can get hit with things that are just unspeakable. Or that leaves us drastically different afterwards. But as long as we have the ability to move on, we might as well try our best.

So, let's also consider this chapter, "Earn your black belt in being awesome." Because that's what this is all about. Living an awesome life and doing awesome things. That can happen on whatever scale you are living your life on. The decision is ultimately yours, based on you choosing to use the cards that you've been dealt properly.

## PERSONAL GROWTH

You have to evolve. Things that don't evolve end up dying out. Evolve in your life. Ask more of yourself, push yourself harder, be honest with yourself about what your faults are, and turn them into your new strength. Take responsibility for your emotions and your actions and make the effort to be better.

## ORGANIZATION

When you have a game plan, when you have things set out and ready for yourself, you can make things move smoothly. Get organized. It can be as simple as using a calendar, programming reminders in your phone, or setting 50 alarms that remind you to do things. But get your life organized and get efficient.

## RELATIONSHIPS

Make an effort with the people that are important to you. It doesn't matter if your circle is small or large, but if people are important to you, show them that. If you're married, never stop dating your spouse. Put in the effort. Be kind to people that you meet because you never know who could be your future friend, client, or employer. Even if you're not a people person, sometimes you've got to be.

## PARENTING

Possibly the most important job you'll ever have. So put the effort into it. Develop a relationship with your children, but also give them room to grow. Remember that they are not growing up the same way that we did. It's a different time and era, so don't be afraid to adjust with the times and just do your best. You're going to make mistakes and that's OK, but keep putting in the effort.

## BUSINESS

Put in the work. That's all there is to it. Whether it's your business or a company you work for, do right by you and do your best. Always know your value. If you're putting in that consistent maximum effort then you know that your value was great. Educate yourself. There's always more for you to learn. Knowledge really is power, so arm yourself with it. Your knowledge combined with your effort and drive can take you far. Take advantage of opportunities and be OK with falling short sometimes. The path to success can sometimes be paved with failure.

## LEADERSHIP

The person that puts in the effort is sometimes a leader whether they mean to be or not. So, if you're trying to improve in all these areas and your hard work is there, you are already leading by example. Don't be afraid to be a communicator, don't be afraid to be the person that steps up and wants to do things, this is what a leader does. You have a responsibility to yourself to live a great life and work hard. You have a responsibility to others when you are setting this example. Make it a good one.

## SUCCESS

Want more. Do more. Be more. The success you achieve is only limited by your ambition and drive. So commit to whatever it is that you're doing. Commit all these concepts from above. No, it's not always going to work out perfectly, but continuing to push and drive forward will get you to a better place. Consistency is key in everything. Things might not happen every time, but if you are consistent then you're going to grow. Be your own definition of success. Don't fit someone else's mold, but fit your own. And make those standards high.

## EARN IT

I like to remind my black belts that "you are only as good as your last class." You can earn a black belt one day and be amazing, and then put in little to no effort for your next 20 classes. Are you really still a black belt? If you're not using the skills that you've earned and trying to apply them to be a better person then you're missing the whole point of the rank. It's the same with everything we've discussed. If you are going to put in the effort to do something, give it your all, and keep at it, even after you've made the progress you wanted. Respect your own sacrifice.

So, I hope that as we've gone on this journey together you really have stopped to think about the things I've brought up. You stopped to ask yourself questions. Gotten some thoughts or inspiration. Or if you disagree with something then it at least helped you think about why you did. Take these lessons and apply them. Make your own decisions and take responsibility for the areas you want to grow in. Put in the effort to earn that black belt in the areas that you choose. Do so with thought, purpose, and integrity. I hope one day to meet you, and shake your hand, and congratulate you on the steps you've taken.

## GO EARN THAT BLACK BELT.

# MY JOURNEY

## NOTES

_____

_____

_____

_____

_____

_____

_____

_____

_____

_____

_____

_____

_____

_____

_____

# ABOUT THE AUTHOR

Robert Nichols has been studying Martial Arts for over 30 years. He is as passionate about learning now as he ever has been. He currently holds ranks in several styles, including 7th degree black belts in Taekwondo and Ninjutsu. He is currently the highest-ranking SAMI Combat Systems instructor in America. A multiple time member of the United States Martial Arts hall of fame as "Instructor of the year" and was voted the 2021 Martial Arts HOF, "Man of the Year." He has also been featured on the cover of the Action Magazine Martial Arts Hall of Honor book twice.

Mr. Nichols has proudly run Union UTA Martial Arts since its opening in 2001. He is available for Public Speaking Engagements on motivation and as a Martial Arts school consultant. He lives in Hunterdon County, New Jersey with his wife and daughter.

## FOLLOW ROBERT NICHOLS AND HIS MARTIAL ARTS PROGRAMS:

Instagram: @robert_nichols_jr, @unionuta @samiunion

Facebook: Robert Nichols, Union UTA Martial Arts, SAMI Combat Systems of NJ

For Information on Speaking Engagements or Martial Arts Consulting visit: www.coachrobertnichols.com and www.unionuta.com

Contact Email: Nichols@unionuta.com